Electric Smoker Cookbook

The Complete Electric Smoker Cookbook - Delicious and Mouthwatering Electric Smoker Recipes

FOR BEGINNERS

Sam Green

Contents

Introduction

The smell of perfectly smoked meat will make your mouth water, and its rich taste will amaze you with the bright notes. Today, you are a lucky owner of the modern Masterbuilt Electric Smoker, so you can smoke any kind of food you like. Do you want to cook chicken wings, turkey breasts or pork ribs in a special way? Now you have an opportunity to prepare smoked food, and it will have an amazing taste, but still be pretty healthy. Instead of buying smoked bacon at the local supermarket, you can cook it by yourself without using harmful preservatives, artificial colors, enormous amounts of the monosodium glutamate, added sugars and other additives.

This cookbook provides you with the numerous delicious recipes and useful tips for using use your Masterbuilt Digital Electric Smoker (models 20072115 and 20071117). When you use this unique and versatile kitchen appliance, it will take your cooking experience to the next level. Digital control system transforms the food preparation process in a simple and enjoyable pastime. You just need to place ingredients inside the smoker and let the appliance do its magic. The end result will amaze even the most refined gourmand.

Masterbuilt Digital Electric Smoker will help you to cook meat, vegetables, beef, pork, seafood, or even herbs and spices in more comfortable and safe way compared to the old-fashioned methods. This modern device was introduced to cater to modern society needs and help you to forget about the complicity of the original smoking process. Today, you can surprise your family and friends with the flavored smoked burgers or corn without putting extreme efforts. All you need is to buy high-quality ingredients, choose an appealing recipe, and power on your Masterbuilt Digital Electric Smoker. Let's stop wasting your time and smoke your first dish right now!

5 Reasons Why You Will Fall In Love with Your Electronic Smoker

Reason #1 – Mind-Blowing Flavor

Using this Masterbuilt Digital Electric Smoker, you will never be disappointed with the result: every piece of the meat and poultry will be an indulgence of rich taste and aroma. Meats will be tender and easy to chew, so it will literally melt in your mouth. At the same time, your smoked food will also look as good as it tastes, which will make your appetite stronger and your enjoyment in your food so much more. Your homemade smoked sausages, pork ribs and chicken wings will be real stars like meals posted on social media.

Reason #2 – Time-Saving Cooking

If you love the smoked meals, but have no time for cooking, then Masterbuilt Digital Electric Smoker is here to the rescue. You can simply place the ingredients inside the electric smoker, then carry on with your day-to-day activities. You can spend your spare time binge-watching TV shows or playing with your kids in the yard. After few hours, you will be able to enjoy aromatic and delicious meal right at your dinner table. There is no sense to become stuck in the kitchen when you have an opportunity to prepare yummy dishes without any efforts.

Reason #3 – User-Friendly Control

The electric smokers are modern day inventions that have user-friendly digital control. Today's electric mechanisms monitor the temperate during the cooking process and make it possible to adjust the temperature for cooking certain food. Masterbuilt 20072115 is one of the smartest electronic smokers in the market; it can be turned on and off via Bluetooth. The wireless connectivity to the app allow you to cook stress-free throughout this otherwise complex process.

Reason #4 – Durable and Safe Construction

The basic construction of the electric smoker is very durable. The design and the material used to build the electric smoker are mostly of stainless steel, which makes it dust- and rust-resistant, as well as lightweight. For this reason, it can be assembled and moved from place to place with ease. Moreover, Masterbuilt machine is safe to use with a reduced risk of electric shock or burning from some drippings.
Overall, the construction of this cooking device is close to perfection: the integrated thermostat controls the temperature for even and consistent smoking and helps create an ideal bark.

Reason #5 – Compact Size

Electric smoker is only 30-inch high, so a huge space or designated backyard area is not required to be constructed just to hold a smoker. The Masterbuilt smoker allows you to smoke the food right beside the kitchen. While electric smoker looks compact, it is actually pretty spacious inside, so it is suitable for the large family meal preparation. It fits up to 6 whole chickens, 4 pork butts or 64 sausages.

How to Use an Electric Smoker

Using an electric smoker is not a complex process; you just put the meat into the smoker and fire it up. The cooking process is very basic; you wear gloves for safety and then add the wood chip to the smoker. You can take out the tray and put chips directly. Once the smoking process has started, you can add more additional chips in the side to build up and maintain enough smoke. This process helps infuse smoke into the food.

Once you have the chips in place, it is time to put meat or other food items onto the grill. The grills are capable of cooking the way gas grills cook. You can place aluminum foil sheets or trays in the last chamber of a smoker to collect any dripping from the food. Lock the door of the smoker and let the cooking process begin. The food digital controller helps to adjust the temperature and time with the push of the button. So sit back, relax and enjoy.

3 Tips to Get Perfectly Smoked Food

1.   CHOOSE THE BEST QUALITY INGREDIENTS. The better meat, poultry and vegetables you use, the the better your smoked meals will get. Don't be surprised that smoked sausages are not good enough because you purchased a cheaper, lower quality product.

2.   CLEAN THE SMOKER AFTER EVERY USAGE. The racks are removable and they can be taken out to clean the inner chamber easily. If food is smoked in a dirty machine, it can leave a bitter aftertaste.

3.   USE AN APPROPRIATE KIND OF THE CHIP WOOD. Keep in mind that Hickory chips are great for most meats, while apple wood should be better used for chicken and pork. Mesquite adds great flavor to beef while alder is ideal for fish.

chapter one

Pork Recipes

Delicious Pork Loin Recipe

Prep Time: 1 Hour • Cooking Time: 3 Hours • Servings: 6

Ingredients:

4 pounds of pork loin, whole boneless

1 tablespoon of five-spice powder

Sea salt, to taste

Black pepper, to taste

1 teaspoon of garlic powder

½ teaspoon of nutmeg

2 tablespoons of safflower oil

Apple juice (as needed)

Water, as needed

Directions:

— First, rinse the pork loin and pat dry with a paper towel. Trim the excess fat from the loin. Transfer the pork loin to a sheet pan.

— Take a small bowl and combine five-spice powder, salt, pepper, garlic powder, and nutmeg. Then add oil to it and make a paste.

— Rub this prepared paste all over the loin and let it sit at room temperature for 60 minutes.

— Afterward, preheat the electric smoker to 225 degrees F.

— Place water and apple juice in a bowl at the base of the electric smoker.

— Now add wood chips to the side tray of the electric smoker. Then place the pork loin, fat side up, on the middle rack. Next, insert the probe thermometer, for heat measurements.

— Close the electric smoker door and then cook for 3 hours.

— Check the pork loin every 45 minutes for an internal temperature of 180°F.

— Add more wood chips if the smoke is not enough.
— Add water and apple juice if needed.
— Now remove the pork from the electric smoker and place it on a cutting board. Allow the meat to rest for about 15 minutes before cutting.
— Slice it thinly and serve it with your favorite's salad or side serving.

Nutrition Facts per serving:

Calories 1159 and Daily Value*
Total Fat 67.8g 87%
Saturated Fat 24.1g 120%
Cholesterol 363mg 121%
Sodium 334mg 15%
Total Carbohydrate 5.1g 2%

Dietary Fiber 0.2g 1%
Total Sugars 4.2g
Protein 124g
Calcium 102mg 8%
Iron 4mg 22%
Potassium 1970mg

Honey And Maple Glazed Ham In An Electric Smoker

Prep Time: 30 Minutes • Cooking Time: 3 Hours 40 Minutes • Servings: 4

Ingredients:

4 pounds of boneless ham, spiral sliced

Glaze:

⅓ cup of maple syrup
½ cup of spicy honey
½ cup dark brown sugar
¼ cup ground red pepper
¼ cup apple juice

¼ teaspoon minced ginger
¼ teaspoon cinnamon
¼ teaspoon allspice powder
¼ teaspoon garlic powder

Directions:

— First, preheat the electric smoker grill to 225 degrees F.
— Take a small cooking pot and heat it over medium flame.

— Now add all the ingredients of glaze to the cooking pot and let it cook for about 5 minutes.
— Once the sugar dissolves, the glaze is ready.
— Now place the ham in a casserole dish, cut side down.
— Drizzle half of the glaze over the ham and brush it for even coating.
— Cover the ham with aluminum foil tightly.
— Place the casserole dish on a middle rack of electric smoker and cook it for 3½ hours.
— Afterward, remove the ham from the electric smoker.
— After removing the aluminum foil, drain off the juices.
— At this stage, apply the reserved glaze over the ham.
— Replace wood chips with new fresh ones.
— When smoke gets heavy, put the ham back in the smoker uncovered.
— Let it cook for 10 more minutes.
— Remove the ham from the electric smoker; let it sit for 20 minutes.
— Then, slice and serve.

Nutrition Facts per serving:

Calories 1781 and Daily Value*

Total Fat 78.1g 100%

Saturated Fat 26.7g 133%

Cholesterol 517mg 172%

Sodium 11835mg 515%

Total Carbohydrate 115g 42%

Dietary Fiber 12.1g 43%

Total Sugars 77.3g

Protein 150.9g

Calcium 242mg 19%

Iron 10mg 55%

Potassium 2714mg 58%

Pork Tenderloin Recipe

Prep Time: 30 Minutes • Cooking Time: 2-3 Hours • Servings: 5

Ingredients for Sauce:

2 cups ketchup

½ cup dark brown sugar

4 tablespoons apple cider vinegar

2 tbsps Worcestershire sauce

2 teaspoons BBQ sauce

Salt, to taste

Ground black pepper, to taste

½ teaspoon garlic powder

½ teaspoon of chopped onion

2 tablespoons apple juice

Ingredients for Dry Rub:

Kosher salt, to taste

2 tsp garlic pepper seasoning

Meat and Rolls:

2 pork tenderloins (4 pounds), remove the silver skin

Butter substitute spray

16 sweet Hawaiian rolls

Directions:

— Preheat the electric smoker to 225 degrees F.

— Take a saucepan and heat all the sauce ingredients in it for about 6 minutes.

— Once it's done, let it cool aside for further use.

— Now in a separate bowl, mix together the dry rub ingredients.

— Take tenderloins and fold the thin edges under the tenderloins and tie it with a string. Season the tenderloins with the rub.

— Grease the tenderloins with the butter spray.

— Add wood chips to the side tray of the electric smoker. Place the pork tenderloins on the middle rack.

— Cook until the thermometer read 205 degrees F of internal temperature.

— Remove the pork from the grill and allow resting for 5 minutes.

— Slice the tenderloin, and place between toasted buns or rolls.

— Drizzle with prepared sauce and serve.

Nutrition Facts per serving:

.Calories 1100 and Daily Value*

Total Fat 29.9g 38%

Saturated Fat 10.2g 51%

Cholesterol 284mg 95%

Sodium 1744mg 76%

Total Carbohydrate 99.9g 36%

Dietary Fiber 2.9g 10%

Total Sugars 46.7g

Protein 102.7g

Calcium 206mg 16%

Iron 9mg 48%

Potassium 1870mg 40%

Smoked Pork Shoulders

Prep Time: 8 Hour • Cooking Time: 12 Hours • Servings: 6

Ingredients:

6 pounds pork shoulder, Boston butt

Ingredient For Brine

½ cup molasses
10 ounces pickling salt

6-8 cups of water

Ingredients For The Rub:

2 teaspoons ground cumin
1 teaspoon ground fennel
1 teaspoon coriander

2 tablespoons chili powder
2 tablespoons onion powder
½ tablespoon paprika

Directions:

— Combine molasses, pickling salt, and water in a large bowl to make brine. Put the pork into the brine for about 8 hours before starting the cooking process. Pat dry the meat.

— Apply all the rub ingredients evenly all over the pork.

— Now start the cooking process by adding the wood chips to the smoker.

— Place the meat on the sheet pan and transfer to the top most rack of the smoker.

— Next, insert the probe thermometer for heat measurements inside the meat.

— Close the electric smoker door and then cook for12 hours at 225 degrees F.

— Once the internal temperature reaches 190 degrees F, the meat is done.

— Let the pork rest for 20 to 30 minutes before serving.

Nutrition Facts per serving:

Calories 1449 and Daily Value*
Total Fat 98.9g 127%

Saturated Fat 35.7g 179%
Cholesterol 408mg 136%

Sodium 19261mg 837%

Total Carbohydrate 26.7g 10%

Dietary Fiber 2.6g 9%

Total Sugars 16.2g

Protein 107.6g

Calcium 255mg 20%

Iron 9mg 48%

Potassium 1980mg 42%

Delicious Smoked Pork

Prep Time: 13 Hours • Cooking Time: 4 Hours • Servings: 4-6

Ingredients:

4 pounds pork shoulder

Kosher salt, to taste

2 tablespoons smoked paprika

3 tablespoons lemon Pepper

2 tablespoons cayenne pepper

1 tablespoon garlic powder

1 tablespoon black pepper

½ cup of yellow mustard

4 tbsps of Worcestershire sauce

⅓ cup of apple cider vinegar

1 cup apple juice

½ cup water

Directions:

— First, wash the pork shoulder under hot water, then pat dry.

— In a bowl, combine salt, paprika, lemon pepper, cayenne pepper, garlic powder, and black pepper. Put the pork shoulder on a large cookie sheet.

— Spread the Worcestershire sauce all over the pork and then rub mustard over the shoulder gently.

— Rub the bowl, spice mixture over the pork and then wrap the shoulder with a plastic wrap. Marinate it for 12 hours in a refrigerator.

— After 12 hours have passed, remove the pork shoulder from the fridge and let come to room temperature. Bring the smoker to 220 degrees F.

— Combine apple cider vinegar, water and apple juice in a spray bottle

— Soak smoking chips in water in a bucket by the smoker.

— Place the handful of smoking chips into the smoking basket and place the marinated pork shoulder inside the smoker. Spray it with bottle liquid every 45-60 minutes. Add additional wood chips when needed.

— Cook for about 4 hours. Let it sit for one hour before serving.

Nutrition Facts per serving:

Calories 1430 and Daily Value*

Total Fat 99.4g 127%

Saturated Fat 36g 180%

Cholesterol 408mg 136%

Sodium 876mg 38%

Total Carbohydrate 19.9g 7%

Dietary Fiber 4.7g 17%

Total Sugars 10.5g

Protein 108.7g

Calcium 167mg 13%

Iron 9mg 50%

Potassium 1831mg 39%

Apple Wood Smoked Pork Loin In A Digital Smoker

Prep Time: 1 Hour • Cooking Time: 5 Hours • Servings: 6

Ingredients:

5 pounds of pork loin, trimmed

2 tablespoons canola oil

3 tablespoons garlic powder

2 tablespoons dried rosemary, chopped

¼ cup salt, or to taste

½ cup dry pistachios, chopped and roasted

6 tablespoons ground black peppercorns

Directions:

— Load the electric smoker grill with apple wood chips and preheat it for 50 minutes at 225 degrees F.

— Rinse and pat dry the pork and then brush it with oil.

— Now rub all the listed spice over the pork and then let the pork rest for 10 minutes.

— Next, insert the probe thermometer for heat measurements inside the meat.

— Close the electric smoker door and then cook for 3-5 hours until internal temperate reaches 200 degrees F.

— The pork is done, take it out and let it sit for a few minutes before serving.

Nutrition Facts per serving:

Calories 1167 and Daily Value*

Total Fat 68.1g 87%

Saturated Fat 24.2g 121%

Cholesterol 363mg 121%

Sodium 301mg 13%

Total Carbohydrate 7.9g 3%

Dietary Fiber 2g 7%

Total Sugars 1.1g

Protein 125.1g

Calcium 121mg 9%

Iron 6mg 31%

Potassium 2026mg 43%

Stuffed Smoked Pork Tenderloin

Prep Time: 65 Minutes • Cooking Time: 2-3 Hours • Servings: 6

Ingredients:

2 pounds of 2 pork tenderloins, trimmed

½ cup of prosciutto, thin slices

¼ cup fresh bread crumbs

3 tablespoons fresh parsley, minced

1 teaspoon fresh rosemary, minced

2 cloves of garlic, minced

4 tablespoons extra virgin olive oil

Salt and black pepper to taste

Directions:

— Preheat the smoker to 225 degrees F for 40 minutes, by adding the cherry wood chip into the smoker box.

— Take a cutting board and place the two tenderloins on it.

— Place the prosciutto slices over one of the tenderloins, so it hangs from all the sides.

— In a separate bowl, combine the bread crumbs, rosemary, parsley, and garlic.

— Place it over the prosciutto.

— Lay tenderloin on top, and then ties it with kitchen string.

— Transfer the tenderloin on a rimmed foil-lined baking sheet.

— Place the tenderloin inside the smoker. Attach the digital thermometer for reading the temperate.

— Smoke until it reaches the internal temperature of 205 degrees F.
— Let the tenderloin rest 20 minutes before removing the string.
— Then slice and serve.

Nutrition Facts per serving:

Calories 477 and Daily Value*

Total Fat 19.6g 25%

Saturated Fat 4.8g 24%

Cholesterol 145mg 48%

Sodium 1424mg 62%

Total Carbohydrate 18g 7%

Dietary Fiber 0.4g 1%

Total Sugars 10.4g

Protein 58.2g

Calcium 37mg 3%

Iron 4mg 20%

Potassium 1680mg 36%

Smoked Pork Chops with Apple and Onion Compote

Prep Time: 80 Minutes • Cooking Time: 4 hours • Servings: 4

Ingredients:

4 boneless pork chops

½ cup of BBQ Rub

2 tablespoons canola oil

2 tablespoons water

2 Spanish onions

2 apples, Granny Smith

2 tablespoons butter

¼ teaspoon cinnamon

½ teaspoon dry mustard

⅓ teaspoon nutmeg

Salt and pepper, to taste

Directions:

— Preheat the electric smoker and place apple wood chips in the smoke box. Let it heat for about 50 minutes.

— Meanwhile, season the pork chops with BBQ rub by placing it on a baking sheet. Then, covered it with the aluminum foil.

— Set the temperature of the preheated smoker to 225 degrees F.

— Insert the digital thermometer in the thickest part of the pork chop.

- Set the internal temperate to 200 degrees F.
- Place baking sheet with the chop into the smoker.
- Smoke the chops for about 4 hours.
- Meanwhile, make the compote by adding oil to the skillet and heat it over the low flame. Now add onion and cook until soft.
- It took about 15 minutes at low heat. Take out the onion and add apples with water, and cook until turn golden.
- Melt the butter in the same pan and add cinnamon, dry mustard, and nutmeg. Add onions back to the pan and mix well.
- Season it with salt and pepper. Once chops are cooked, serve it with prepared compote.

Nutrition Facts per serving:

Calories 416 and Daily Value*

Total Fat 26.2g 34%

Saturated Fat 9.2g 46%

Cholesterol 70mg 23%

Sodium 1078mg 47%

Total Carbohydrate 21.9g 8%

Dietary Fiber 4.1g 14%

Total Sugars 14g

Protein 26.1g

Calcium 19mg 1%

Iron 1mg 4%

Potassium 205mg 4%

Sweet and Spicy Pork Shoulder

Prep Time: 120 Minutes • Cooking Time: 4 Hours • Servings: 6

Ingredients:

4 pounds pork shoulder, roasts

Shoulder Rub Ingredients:

¼ cup brown sugar

½ cup white sugar

½ cup paprika

⅓ cup garlic powder

1 tablespoon chili powder

1 teaspoon cayenne pepper

1 teaspoon dried oregano

1 teaspoon cumin

Injection Liquid Ingredients:

¾ cup apple juice

½ cup water

½ cup sugar

3 tablespoons salt

2 tablespoons Worcestershire sauce

Directions:

— Combine all the rub ingredients in a large bowl.

— In a separate bowl, combine all the liquid ingredients.

— Inject the liquid into the meat using the injector.

— Pat dry the top surface of the meat, and then rub the spice mix all over meat evenly.

— Let the meat sit for 2 hours at room temperature.

— Cook it in an electric smoker for 4 hours, at 225 degrees F.

— Serve and enjoy.

Nutrition Facts per serving:

Calories 998 and Daily Value*

Total Fat 63g 81%

Saturated Fat 21.7g 108%

Cholesterol 214mg 71%

Sodium 3755mg 163%

Total Carbohydrate 54.9g 20%

Dietary Fiber 4.4g 16%

Total Sugars 45.9g

Protein 53.6g

Calcium 42mg 3%

Iron 6mg 32%

Potassium 348mg 7%

Smoked Pork Crown Roast with Pan Gravy

Prep Time: 2 Hours • Cooking Time: 8 Hours • Servings: 12

Ingredients:

8 pounds crown roast of pork

Salt and pepper, to taste

10 garlic cloves, minced

4 tablespoons honey Dijon mustard

2 tablespoons apple cider vinegar

2 tablespoons dark brown sugar

A handful of fresh sage

Ingredients for The Gravy:

1 cup butter

6 cloves garlic, minced

¼ cup flour

½ cup white wine

⅓ cup of chicken broth

3 tablespoons fresh parsley, minced

Salt and black pepper

Directions:

— Grind the trimmings of the meat crown.

— Preheat the electric smoker to 225 degrees F for about 30 minutes.

— Place the rack in the lowest position.

— Fill the water pan for the wood chips.

— Season the pork with salt and pepper.

— Rest it for one hour at room temperature.

— When the electric smoker is heated, start with the cooking process.

— In a bowl, combine minced garlic, Dijon honey mustard, apple cider vinegar, and sugar.

— Brush the mixture well over the pork.

— Adjust the digital thermometer inside any meat part.

— Place the crown pork roast in the electric smoker.

— Cook it until the temperate reading is 180-200 degrees F.

— Remove the pork from smoker and preheat the gas grill.

— Finish it over the grill flames for a more texture outer layer.

— Meanwhile, prepare the gravy by heating butter in a large skillet over medium heat.

— Add the dripping from the pan inside the smoker.

— Add the broth and bring mixture to boil.

— Afterward, reduce heat and let it simmer.

— Add salt, pepper, garlic, flour, white wine, and parsley.

— Place the crown roast on a serving plate and drizzle pan gravy on top.

— You can serve the gravy individually as well.

— Serve with a garnish of fresh sage.

Nutrition Facts per serving:

Calories 810 and Daily Value*

Total Fat 54.2g 70%

Saturated Fat 19.1g 95%

Cholesterol 278mg 93%

Sodium 240mg 10%

Total Carbohydrate 7g 3%

Dietary Fiber 0.2g 1%

Total Sugars 2.6g

Protein 71g

Calcium 14mg 1%

Iron 4mg 23%

Potassium 42mg 1%

Zesty Mustard Smoke Pork Tenderloin in a Smoker

Prep Time: 30 Minutes • Cooking Time: 3 Hours • Servings: 2

Ingredients:

2 pork tenderloins

4 tablespoons of BBQ sauce

Pork Rub Ingredients:

¼ cup cane sugar

¼ teaspoon chili powder

½ tablespoon granulated onion

½ tablespoon granulated garlic

½ tablespoons dried chilies

¼ tablespoon dill weed

½ tablespoon lemon powder

½ tablespoon mustard powder

Directions:

— Combine all the rub ingredients in a large bowl and set aside.

— Start the smoker and add apple wood chips.

— Adjust the setting to 225 degrees F.

— Meanwhile, trim the pork fat and silver skin. Rub the seasoning over the pork loin. Place the pork in the smoker.

— Cook for 3 hours until internal temperate reaches 200 degrees F.

— Brush the BBQ sauce on the pork and then left it to sit for 20 minutes.

— Then serve and enjoy.

Nutrition Facts per serving:

Calories 894 and Daily Value*

Total Fat 33.4g 43%

Saturated Fat 8.2g 41%

Cholesterol 300mg 100%

Sodium 2164mg 94%

Total Carbohydrate 41g 15%

Dietary Fiber 1.3g 5%

Total Sugars 16.8g

Protein 98.7g

Calcium 111mg 9%

Iron 7mg 41%

Potassium 563mg 12%

Balsamic BBQ Sauce with Glazed Baby Back Ribs

Prep Time: 40 Minutes • Cooking Time: 4 Hours • Servings: 4

Ingredients for The Rub:

1 tablespoon dark brown sugar

3 tablespoons kosher salt, or to taste

½ tablespoon granulated sugar

2 tablespoons paprika

⅓ teaspoon ground white pepper

1 teaspoon ground black pepper

1 teaspoon ground mustard

⅓ teaspoon dried thyme

½ teaspoon garlic powder

½ teaspoon ground Szechuan peppercorns

⅓ teaspoon cayenne pepper

Other Ingredients:

2 racks baby back ribs

1-½ cups balsamic barbecue sauce

Directions:

— Combine all the rub ingredients in a large bowl and set aside.

— Start the smoker and add apple wood. Adjust the setting to 225 degrees F.

— Add the chunk of wood when at this temperature.

— Season the rib with the rub and set aside for a few minutes.

— Once, the wood starts giving smoke, place the ribs inside the smoker.

— Cook for 4 hours. When one hour left base the top of the ribs with the BBQ sauce. Continue to cook until caramelized.

Nutrition Facts per serving:

Calories 883 and Daily Value*
Total Fat 42.5g 54%
Saturated Fat 17g 85%
Cholesterol 262mg 87%
Sodium 6200mg 270%
Total Carbohydrate 31.5g 11%

Dietary Fiber 2.1g 8%
Total Sugars 20.5g
Protein 90.4g
Calcium 65mg 5%
Iron 10mg 56%
Potassium 1526mg 32%

Pork Shoulder Steaks Recipe

Prep Time: 30 Minutes • Cooking Time: 7 Hour 30 Minutes • Servings: 10

Ingredients for The Char Siu Sauce:

½ cup hoisin sauce
⅓ cup honey
½ cup soy sauce

¼ cup dry sherry
3 teaspoons Chinese five-spice powder

Ingredients for Rub:

4 tablespoons five-spice powder
2 tablespoons dark brown sugar

2 tablespoons sea salt, or to taste

Meat Includs:

7 pounds of 1 boneless pork Boston butt

Directions:

— Whisk together all the sauce ingredients to make a sauce in medium bowl.
— To prepare a rub, take a separate bowl and combine all the rub ingredients.
— Rub the seasoning all over the pork butt meat.
— Coat evenly and then place it in a resealed plastic bag.
— Now, turn on the smoker and adjust it out 255 degrees F.
— Then add wood chips and wait once the wood starts producing smoke.
— Now, place the meat inside the smoker and then smoke it for 7 hours.

— Meanwhile, pour all the sauce ingredients into the saucepan and bring the mixture to boil. Reduce heat of the pan to low and simmer for 10 minutes.

— Once thickened, turn the heat off.

— Once the pork cooked, brush sauce over the meat evenly.

— Continue to smoke it for 30 more minutes. Serve when done.

Nutrition Facts per serving:

Calories 695 and Daily Value*

Total Fat 21.6g 28%

Saturated Fat 7.1g 36%

Cholesterol 292mg 97%

Sodium 1104mg 48%

Total Carbohydrate 18g 7%

Dietary Fiber 1.1g 4%

Total Sugars 14.7g

Protein 100.4g

Calcium 66mg 5%

Iron 4mg 24%

Potassium 1248mg 27%

Beer Pork Steak

Prep Time: 1hour 30 Minutes • Cooking Time: 2 Hours • Servings: 4

Ingredients:

4 pork shoulder steaks

1 cup of BBQ sauce

1 can of beer of your choice

Oil spray, for greasing

Ingredients for The Rub:

6 tablespoons paprika

Salt, to taste

Black pepper, to taste

4 tablespoons brown sugar

3 tablespoons garlic powder

2 tablespoons onion powder

Directions:

— Preheat the electric smoker to 225 degrees F for 30 minutes by adding apple wood chips.

— To start cooking, first, combine all the rub ingredients in a bowl to prepare a rub. Rub the steaks with the prepared rub well and then marinate for 30 minutes in the refrigerator.

— Combine the beer and BBQ sauce in a small bowl.

— Brush the steak with BBQ sauce mix and place inside the smoker for cooking for about 45 minutes.

— After 10 minutes of cooking, brush with more BBQ sauce mixture to the pork steak to keep it moist. Cook for additional 45 minutes at 325 degrees F.

— Once the internal temperature reaches 185 degrees F, the steak is ready to be served.

— Take the steak out of the electric smoker and then serve with more BBQ sauce if liked.

Nutrition Facts per serving:

Calories 515 and Daily Value*

Total Fat 17.9g 23%

Saturated Fat 6.4g 32%

Cholesterol 122mg 41%

Sodium 824mg 36%

Total Carbohydrate 47.8g 17%

Dietary Fiber 5.1g 18%

Total Sugars 28.8g

Protein 35.8g

Calcium 85mg 7%

Iron 5mg 29%

Potassium 899mg 19%

Cherry-Spiced Maple Glazed Ham

Prep Time: 1 Hour • Cooking Time: 2-3 Hours • Servings: 3

Sauce Ingredients:

1 cup cherry preserves

⅓ cup light brown sugar, packed

⅓ cup maple syrup

½ cup water

1-ounce honey whiskey

2 tablespoons Dijon mustard

1 teaspoon cinnamon

Cayenne pepper, to taste

1 teaspoon ground cloves

½ teaspoon garlic powder

2 tablespoons butter

Other Ingredients:

2 pounds of spiral cut ham

Kosher salt and black pepper, to taste

Ingredients for Basting

2 tablespoons of canola oil   4-6 ounces of cherry juice

Directions:

— Combine all the glaze ingredients in a pot, and let it cook for a few minutes until sugar dissolved.
— Then set aside for further use.
— You can puree it in a blender after cooling, for a fine consistency.
— Add more water if the consistency is too thick.
— Preheat the smoker for 20 minutes at 225 degrees F.
— Combine cherry juice and 1 tablespoon oil in a separate bowl, which will be used further for basting.
— Drizzle one tablespoon of the reserved oil over the ham and rub well.
— Season the meat with salt and pepper.
— Cook inside the electric smoker for 2-3 hours.
— Keep basting the ham after every 30 minutes with prepared basting mixture.
— When the internal temperature reaches 205 degrees F, the ham is ready.
— Let it sit at room temperature for 30 minutes before serving.
— Brush a final layer of basting mixture, and then serve with prepared sauce as a side serving.
— Enjoy.

Nutrition Facts per serving:

Calories 1247 and Daily Value*   Dietary Fiber 6.2g 22%
Total Fat 43.7g 56%   Total Sugars 107.1g
Saturated Fat 14.5g 73%   Protein 52.6g
Cholesterol 193mg 64%   Calcium 286mg 22%
Sodium 4161mg 181%   Iron 4mg 25%
Total Carbohydrate 162.3g 59%   Potassium 1451mg 31%

chapter two

Chicken Recipes

Herbed and Smoked Chicken

Prep Time: 3 Hours • Cooking Time: 90 Minutes • Servings: 2-3

Ingredients:

15 cups filtered water

4 cups nonalcoholic beer

Salt, to taste

1 cup brown sugar

1 tablespoon rosemary

1 teaspoon sage

2 pounds whole chicken, trimmed and giblets removed

4 tablespoons butter

3 tablespoons olive oil, for basting

1 cup Italian seasoning

2 tablespoons garlic powder

Zest of 3 small lemons

Directions:

— Add water to a large cooking pot, then add salt and sugar.

— Let it boil until dissolved.

— Add the herbs and let it cook for a few minutes until aromatic.

— Pour in the beer and then immerse chicken in it.

— Let it refrigerate for a few hours.

— Now, remove the chicken from the brine, and then pat dry with a paper towel.

— Uncover and let it sit for one more hour in room temperate.

— Next, butter the chicken.

— Massage the chicken for fine coating.

— Next, rub the chicken with Italian seasoning, garlic powder, and lemon zest.

— Load electric smoker with the wood chips, and preheat to 250 degrees F until smoke starts to build.

— Then, slow roast it for 1.5 hours to 2 hours, and keep basting with olive oil every 30 minutes.

— Once, the internal temperature reaches 165 degrees F and juices run clear, serve and enjoy.

Nutrition Facts per serving:

Calories 1284 and Daily Value*

Total Fat 74.2g 95%

Saturated Fat 21.5g 107%

Cholesterol 362mg 21%

Sodium 461mg 20%

Total Carbohydrate 65g 24%

Dietary Fiber 1g 4%

Total Sugars 53.6g

Protein 88.6g

Calcium 119mg 9%

Iron 5mg 27%

Potassium 861mg 18%

Smoked Chicken Thighs

Prep Time: 2 Hours 10 Minutes • Cooking Time: 90 Minutes • Servings: 2

Ingredients:

2 pounds chicken thighs

6 tablespoons soy sauce

3 teaspoons sesame oil

4 garlic cloves

4 scallions

1 tablespoon thyme

1 teaspoon allspice

⅓ teaspoon cinnamon

⅓ teaspoon crushed red pepper

Directions:

— Combine soy sauce and oil in a bowl and rub it gently over the chicken thighs.

— In a food processor, blend together garlic, scallion, thyme, cinnamon, allspice, and red pepper.

— Blend it until smooth.

— Rub it all over the thighs and seal the chick in the zip-lock plastic bag.

— Let it marinate for about 2 hours.

— Preheat smoker to 250 degrees F, by adding the cherry wood to the smoker, and let wait for the smoke to release. Smoke the chicken for 90 minutes.
— Adjust the thermometer to read the internal temperate.
— Once the internal temperature reaches 165 degrees F. Serve it and enjoy.

Nutrition Facts per serving:

Calories 974 and Daily Value*

Total Fat 40.8g 52%

Saturated Fat 10.3g 52%

Cholesterol 404mg 135%

Sodium 3103mg 135%

Total Carbohydrate 9.9g 4%

Dietary Fiber 2.3g 8%

Total Sugars 1.6g

Protein 135.4g

Calcium 146mg 11%

Iron 9mg 49%

Potassium 1342mg 29%

BBQ Chicken Wings Recipe

Prep Time: 2 Hours • Cooking Time: 2 Hours • Servings: 4

Ingredients:

4 pounds turkey wings
1 cup of BBQ sauce

Directions:

— Cut the chicken wings and discard the tips.
— Marinate the wings in the BBQ sauce for about 2 hours.
— Now preheat the smoker for a few minutes at 250 degrees F.
— Add the cherry wood chip to the smoker and let the smoker release smoke.
— Place the chicken into the smoker.
— Cook for two hours or until the internal temperature reaches 165 degrees F.
— Use the digital meat thermometer to measure the temperature.

Nutrition Facts per serving:

Calories 276 and Daily Value*

Total Fat 10.2g 13%

Saturated Fat 0g 0%

Cholesterol 0mg 0%

Sodium 699mg 30%

Protein 23g

Total Carbohydrate 22.7g 8%

Calcium 8mg 1%

Dietary Fiber 0.4g 1%

Iron 0mg 1%

Total Sugars 16.3g

Potassium 130mg 3%

Lemon Garlic Chicken Breast Recipe

Prep Time: 2 Hours • Cooking Time: 90 Minutes • Servings: 2

Ingredients:

2-pound chicken breasts, boneless and skinless

4 cloves minced garlic

2-inches ginger, minced

4 lemons, juice only

4 tablespoons olive oil

Salt, to taste

Black pepper, to taste

1 teaspoon turmeric

Directions:

— Take a bowl and combine salt, pepper, lemon juice, olive oil, turmeric, ginger, and garlic in a bowl. Mix well and rub the chicken with the prepared mix. Let the chicken marinate for 2 hours in the refrigerator.

— Now preheat the smoker to 250 degrees F.

— Add the cherry wood chip to the smoker and let the smoke release.

— Place the chicken into the smoker. Cook for 90 minutes or until the internal temperature reaches 165 F.

— Use the digital meat thermometer to measure the temperature.

Nutrition Facts per serving:

Calories 1155 and Daily Value*

Dietary Fiber 3.9g 14%

Total Fat 62.2g 80%

Total Sugars 3.1g

Saturated Fat 13.4g 67%

Protein 133.1g

Cholesterol 404mg 135%

Calcium 113mg 9%

Sodium 472mg 21%

Iron 7mg 39%

Total Carbohydrate 14.8g 5%

Potassium 1339mg

Balsamic Vinegar Chicken Breasts

Prep Time: 3 Hours • Cooking Time: 2 Hours • Servings: 2

Ingredients:

4 tablespoons olive oil

½ cup balsamic vinegar

4 cloves garlic, minced

2 tablespoons basil, fresh

1 teaspoon red chili powder

Salt and black pepper, to taste

2 pounds chicken breasts, boneless and skinless

Directions:

— Take a zipper-lock plastic bag and combine all the ingredients except chicken. Place the chicken in the bag and let it marinate in the refrigerators for 2 hours.

— Now preheat the smoker for a few minutes at 250 degrees F and add cherry or apple wood chip to the smoker.

— Place the chicken into the smoker once the smoke started to come out.

— Cook until the internal temperature reaches 165 degrees F.

— Use the digital meat thermometer to measure the temperature.

Nutrition Facts per serving:

Calories 1128 and Daily Value*

Total Fat 61.9g 79%

Saturated Fat 13.3g 67%

Cholesterol 404mg 135%

Sodium 407mg 18%

Total Carbohydrate 3.4g 1%

Dietary Fiber 0.6g 2%

Total Sugars 0.4g

Protein 131.9g

Calcium 92mg 7%

Iron 6mg 33%

Potassium 1203mg 26%

Five-Spice Maple Chicken

Prep Time: 2 Hours 20 Minutes • Cooking Time: 2 Hours • Servings: 3

Rub Ingredients:

Black pepper and salt, to taste

4 garlic cloves, minced

2 teaspoons onion powder

2 teaspoons ginger, minced

1 teaspoon five-spice powder

Other Ingredients:

2 pounds whole chicken

2 tablespoons melted butter

1 cup grapefruit juice

2 cups chicken stock

Ingredients for The Maple Glaze:

4 teaspoons coconut milk

2 tablespoons sesame oil

4 tablespoons maple syrup

2 tablespoons lemon juice

2 tablespoons melted butter

Directions:

— First, prepare the glaze by taking a small cooking pot and heat coconut milk in it.

— Then add sesame oil, maple syrup, lemon juice, and melted butter.

— Cook for few minutes and reserve for further use.

— Take a large cooking pot and add the chicken stock and grapefruit juice, let it simmer for a few minutes.

— Submerge the chicken in this liquid and let sit for a few hours.

— Combine all the rub ingredients in a separate bowl.

— Take the chicken out of the liquid and then rub it with prepared rub mixture.

— Preheat the smoker for a few minutes at 250 degrees F.

— Add cherry or apple wood chip to the smoker.

— Place the chicken into the smoker.

— Cook for about 2 hours.

— After every 30 minutes, baste the chicken with the maple glaze.

— Use the digital meat thermometer to measure the temperature.

— Serve and enjoy with the final brush of glaze over the chicken and butter on top.

— Enjoy.

Nutrition Facts per serving:

Calories 930 and Daily Value*

Total Fat 49.1g 63%

Saturated Fat 18.8g 94%

Cholesterol 310mg 103%

Sodium 886mg 39%

Total Carbohydrate 29g 11%

Dietary Fiber 2.1g 7%

Total Sugars 22.8g

Protein 89.7g

Calcium 103mg 8%

Iron 4mg 25%

Potassium 987mg

Spicy Sriracha Chicken Wings Recipe

Prep Time: 40 Minutes • Cooking Time: 2 Hours • Servings: 2

Ingredients:

2 pounds chicken wings

2 teaspoons garlic powder

Sea salt, to taste

Freshly ground black pepper, to taste

2 teaspoons fresh cilantro leaves, minced

Ingredients for The Sauce:

⅓ cup raw honey

⅓ cup Sriracha sauce

2 tablespoons coconut amino

3 limes, juice

Directions:

— Combine all the sauce ingredients in a separate bowl and set aside for further use.

— Season the chicken with garlic, salt, and pepper.

— Preheat the smoker for a few minutes at 250 degrees F.

— Add cherry or apple wood chip to the smoker.

— Place the chicken into the smoker once the smoke starts to come out.

— Close the door and cook for about 2 hours.
— Cook until the internal temperature reaches 165 degrees F.
— Use the digital meat thermometer to measure the temperature.
— Serve and enjoy with the prepared sauce.
— Enjoy.

Nutrition Facts per serving:

Calories 1791 and Daily Value*

Total Fat 109.2g 140%

Saturated Fat 28g 140%

Cholesterol 368mg 123%

Sodium 1700mg 74%

Total Carbohydrate 111.9g 41%

Dietary Fiber 4.6g 16%

Total Sugars 49.8g

Protein 91.5g

Calcium 130mg 10%

Iron 7mg 38%

Potassium 791mg 17%

Sesame Chicken Wings

Prep Time: 2 Hours • Cooking Time: 2 Hours • Servings: 2

Ingredients:

⅓ cup rice vinegar

3 tablespoons honey

½ cup soy sauce

⅓ cup sesame oil

2 tablespoons garlic sauce

1 tablespoon garlic salt, to taste

12 chicken thighs, skinless, boneless

Directions:

— Combine rice vinegar, honey, soy sauce, sesame oil, chili garlic sauce and salt in a small bowl, then coat the chicken thighs with the mixture.
— Refrigerate it for few hours.
— Preheat the smoker for 30 minutes at 255 degrees F.
— Add cherry wood chips to the smoker.
— Place the marinated chicken into the smoker.
— Cook for about 2 hours, or until the internal temperature reaches 165 F.
— Use the digital meat thermometer to measure the temperature.

Nutrition Facts per serving:

Calories 850 and Daily Value*

Total Fat 52.3g 67%

Saturated Fat 3.4g 17%

Cholesterol 0mg 0%

Sodium 2409mg 105%

Total Carbohydrate 23g 8%

Dietary Fiber 0.7g 3%

Total Sugars 18.9g

Protein 79.3g

Calcium 12mg 1%

Iron 1mg 6%

Potassium 134mg 3%

Smoked Apple Wood Chicken Recipe

Prep Time: 3 Hours • Cooking Time: 90 Minutes • Servings: 2

Ingredients:

2 pounds of chicken breasts, split

Ingredients for Marinade:

4 teaspoons barbecue rub

8 tablespoons melted butter

Salt & pepper to taste

Directions:

— Combine BBQ rub and melted butter in a bowl and let it cool at room temperature.

— Take a marinade injector and inject the prepared rub into the chicken breasts.

— You can use a fork to poke the hole in the breasts and then massage the rub gently all over the breasts.

— Prepare your smokers by preheating it to 250 degree F and adding apple wood chips.

— Place the breasts into the smoker.

— Use a digital probe thermometer to read the internal temperature to 165 degrees F.

— Once it reads 165 degrees F, serve.

Nutrition Facts per serving:

Calories 557 and Daily Value*

Total Fat 54.1g 69%

Saturated Fat 29.2g 146%

Cholesterol 122mg 41%

Sodium 349mg 15%

Total Carbohydrate 0.1g 0%

Dietary Fiber 0g 0%

Total Sugars 0g

Protein 22.5g

Calcium 14mg 1%

Iron 0mg 0%

Potassium 14mg 0%

Morocco Smoked Whole Chicken Recipe

Prep Time: 2 Hours • Cooking Time: 3 Hours • Servings: 3

Rub Ingredients:

1 teaspoon fresh cilantro

4 tablespoons olive oil

1 teaspoon garlic powder

1 tablespoon onion powder

1 teaspoon cumin

1 teaspoon paprika

½ teaspoon ground red pepper

1 tablespoon dry lemon zest

Salt, to taste

Other Ingredients:

1 whole chickens, about 2.5 pounds

Directions:

— Combine all the rub ingredients in a small bowl for further use.

— Preheat the smoker to 250 degrees F for 40 minutes by adding cherry wood chips. Rinse the chicken and trim out the excess fat.

— Tie the legs together using a kitchen string.

— Now rub the spice blend over the chicken and then cover for few hours.

— Place the chicken on a baking rack and put it inside the smoker.

— Cook until internal temperate reaches 165 degrees F, about 3 hours

— Take out the chicken and let it sit for few hours before serving.

Nutrition Facts per serving:

Calories 415 and Daily Value*

Total Fat 28g 36%

Saturated Fat 5.2g 26%

Cholesterol 108mg 36%

Sodium 159mg 7%

Total Carbohydrate 5.2g 2%

Dietary Fiber 0.9g 3%

Total Sugars 2.3g

Protein 36.1g

Calcium 38mg 3%

Iron 2mg 13%

Potassium 401mg 9%

Cajun Smoked Chicken Recipe

Prep Time: 20 Minutes • Cooking Time: 4 Hours • Servings: 5

Ingredients:

5 pounds whole chicken

½ cup of Cajun Spice Mix Seasoning, such as from Discovery

Directions:

— Turn the chicken, breast side down.

— Cut along the spine, and remove the backbone from the chicken.

— Press the breast bit down so the chickens get flat.

— Rub the chicken with the Cajun spice mix.

— Place the chicken on a rack. Place the thermometer into the chicken.

— Place it in the electric smoker.

— Fill the wood chip holder with cherry or apple wood chips.

— Fill the water container with water.

— Close the door of the smoker and set the temperature to 250 degrees F.

— Cook until temperature reaches 165 degrees F, or about 4 hours.

— Allow it to come to room temperature, then serve.

Nutrition Facts per serving:

Calories 991 and Daily Value*

Total Fat 72.9g 93%

Saturated Fat 20.1g 101%

Cholesterol 341mg 114%

Sodium 1376mg 60%

Total Carbohydrate 3g 1%

Dietary Fiber 2.5g 9%

Total Sugars 0.4g

Protein 77.7g

Calcium 80mg 6%

Iron 4mg 24%

Potassium 0mg 0%

Herbed Chicken Recipe

Prep Time: 40 Minutes • Cooking Time: 5 Hours • Servings: 6

Ingredients:

6 pounds whole chicken

2 tablespoons dried oregano

2 tablespoons dried thyme

1 tablespoon dried rosemary

1 teaspoon smoked paprika

Salt and pepper, to taste

2 teaspoons garlic powder

3 teaspoons lemon pepper

40 ounces chicken stock

2 carrots, diced

2 celery stalks, diced

2 onions, diced

4 tablespoons dill weed

½ cup extra-virgin olive oil

Directions:

— Preheat the electric smoker to 250 degrees F.

— Combine thyme, oregano, paprika, rosemary, salt, pepper, lemon pepper, and garlic powder in a small bowl.

— Remove all the giblets and neck of the chicken.

— Brush the chicken with the oil, and then massage spices from the bowl all over the chicken

— Pour the stock into a large rack, and lower the spice-rubbed chicken on to the beer.

— Adjust the chicken upright.

— Now, place this rack inside the smoker and toss in the diced veggies onto the rack.

— Let it cook for 5 hours.

— Once, the internal temperate reaches 165 degrees F, the dish is ready.

— Just before 20 minutes remaining, add the dill weeds.

- Then allow cooking for next 20 minutes.
- Carefully remove the rack and then shred the chicken into pieces.
- Mix it with the juices.
- Serve it with orzo pasta.
- Enjoy.

Nutrition Facts per serving:

Calories 1191 and Daily Value*

Total Fat 52.4g 67%

Saturated Fat 12g 60%

Cholesterol 438mg 146%

Sodium 1056mg 46%

Total Carbohydrate 35.8g 13%

Dietary Fiber 3g 11%

Total Sugars 3.5g

Protein 138.6g

Calcium 188mg 14%

Iron 10mg 57%

Potassium 1441mg 31%

Smoked Chicken Quarters

Prep Time: 20 Minutes • Cooking Time: 2 Hours • Servings: 3

Ingredients:

2 cups water

2 teaspoons brown sugar

⅓ cup maple syrup

⅓ cup Sriracha sauce

½ teaspoon salt

⅓ teaspoon pepper

⅓ teaspoon paprika

3 pounds chicken meat

Directions:

- In a large pan, add water along with brown sugar, Sriracha, salt, pepper, paprika, maple syrup, and heat it over the low flame.
- Cook it for 5 minutes.
- Then, once the sugar dissolves, removes it from the heat to let it get cool off.
- Reserve this sauce for later use.
- Set the electric smoker to 250 degrees F. Cook the chicken in it for 2 hours.

— Remember to baste the chicken with the prepared sauce every 20 minutes with a brush.

— Once the digital thermometer meets 165 degrees F, serve with the reserve dripping and remaining sauce.

Nutrition Facts per serving:

Calories 885 and Daily Value*

Total Fat 23.9g 31%

Saturated Fat 5.4g 27%

Cholesterol 359mg 120%

Sodium 797mg 35%

Total Carbohydrate 26.7g 10%

Dietary Fiber 0.2g 1%

Total Sugars 23.8g

Protein 131.5g

Calcium 90mg 7%

Iron 5mg 25%

Potassium 932mg 20%

Orange Sriracha Chicken Legs

Prep Time: 1 Hour • Cooking Time: 2 Hours • Servings: 5

Ingredients:

15 chicken legs

6 tablespoons butter, melted

Ingredient for The Rub:

4 teaspoons sugar

⅓ teaspoon kosher salt

¼ teaspoon black pepper

⅓ teaspoon curry powder

½ teaspoon ground ginger

¼ teaspoon garlic powder

¼ teaspoon Tiger Seasoning

½ teaspoon cinnamon, powder

Ingredients for The Orange Glaze:

1 cup orange marmalade

6 tablespoons chicken stock

2 tablespoons Sriracha

2 tablespoon rice wine vinegar

Directions:

— Preheat the smoker to 250 degrees F for 30 minutes.

— Combine all the rub ingredients in a small bowl.

- Rub the legs of chicken with all the rub ingredients.
- Coat the chicken legs with the melted butter evenly.
- Place the chicken on upper rack of electric smoker and let it cook for 45 minutes.
- Turn the rack every 10 minutes.
- In a small saucepan, mix all the glaze ingredients.
- Bring the mixture to a simmer and whisk it together for 5 minutes.
- Turn the heat off, then strain the sauce.
- After 25 minutes of cooking, baste the legs with orange glaze.
- Cook for 35 more minutes
- Serve.

Nutrition Facts per serving:

Calories 1098 and Daily Value*

Total Fat 59.9g 77%

Saturated Fat 21.5g 107%

Cholesterol 351mg 117%

Sodium 681mg 30%

Total Carbohydrate 47.5g 17%

Dietary Fiber 0.7g 2%

Total Sugars 41.7g

Protein 89.2g

Calcium 74mg 6%

Iron 5mg 26%

Potassium 806mg 17%

Smoked Buffalo Chicken Meatballs

Prep Time: 1 Hour • Cooking Time: 90 Minutes • Servings: 4

Ingredients:

2 pounds ground chicken

3 tablespoons cooked carrot, finely chopped

4 tablespoons celery, finely chopped

2 green onions, finely chopped

⅓ cup dry bread crumbs

⅓ teaspoon salt

⅓ teaspoon paprika

⅓ teaspoon brown sugar

⅓ teaspoon garlic powder

⅓ teaspoon ground black pepper

Ingredients for Ranch Dip:

⅓ cup non-fat Greek yogurt

⅓ cup mayonnaise

2 tablespoon buttermilk

⅓ teaspoon seasoned salt

¼ teaspoon dill

½ teaspoon chili powder

¼ teaspoon granulated garlic

Ingredients for Buffalo Sauce:

½ cup hot sauce

⅓ cup butter

⅓ teaspoon Worcestershire

Directions:

— Combine celery, carrots, chicken, onions and bread crumbs along with salt, sugar, garlic, paprika, and pepper in a bowl.

— Mix well to form the meatballs

— Freeze at least for 30 minutes.

— Combine the entire ranch dip ingredient in a bowl.

— Refrigerate for about 20 minutes.

— Preheat the smoker grill to 250 degrees F.

— Meanwhile, place the hot sauce, butter and Worcestershire sauce in a pot and let it simmer on medium flame.

— Layer meatball in a pan sheet and place the meatballs on the topmost rack and cook for about 30 minutes.

— Turn the meatballs around and then cook for further 10 minutes.

— Once the internal temperature reaches 165 degrees F, take out the meatballs and then toss them in the buffalo sauce glaze.

— Return to the smoker and cook for 50 more minutes.

— Serve it with ranch dip.

Nutrition Facts per serving:

Calories 705 and Daily Value*
Total Fat 39.8g 51%
Saturated Fat 15.7g 79%
Cholesterol 249mg 83%
Sodium 1621mg 70%
Total Carbohydrate 14.5g 5%
Dietary Fiber 1.1g 4%
Total Sugars 4g
Protein 69.6g
Calcium 98mg 8%
Iron 4mg 20%
Potassium 711mg 15%

chapter three
Turkey Recipes

Smoked Turkey

Prep Time: 1 Hour 10 Minutes • Cooking Time: 4 Hours 20 Minutes Servings: 5

Ingredients:

5 pounds turkey, trimmed with giblets removed

1 cup olive oil

5 tablespoons Ras el Hanout

(Moroccan Spice Blend) seasoning

Kosher salt, to taste

Zest of 3 lemons

Mint leaves for garnishing

Directions:

— Cut the backbone of turkey and remove the spine and discard the fat.

— Flip the turkey breast-side up and hand-press into the breastbone to flatten it.

— Rub the turkey with oil and then massage the seasoning along with salt and lemon zest.

— Cover the turkey with plastic wrap and marinate it for 30 minutes.

— Preheat the smoker for 20 minutes.

— Soak the wood chip in water one hour before smoking.

— Remove plastic wrap and cook the turkey for 4 hours 20 minutes at 250 degrees F.

— Garnish it with mint leaves.

Nutrition Facts per serving:

Calories 1062 and Daily Value*

Total Fat 72.7g 93%

Saturated Fat 15.9g 79%

Cholesterol 284mg 95%

Sodium 1660mg 72%

Total Carbohydrate 3.8g 1%

Dietary Fiber 2.2g 8%

Total Sugars 1.5g

Protein 85.2g

Calcium 45mg 3%

Iron 1mg 6%

Potassium 10mg 0%

Turkey with Chimichurri

Prep Time: 1 Hour 10 Minutes • Cooking Time: 4 Hours • Servings: 5

Ingredients:

5 pounds bone-in, skin on turkey pieces

Salt and pepper

1teaspoon paprika

½ teaspoon cayenne

2 tablespoons olive oil

1 pepper

1 onion

2 carrots, chopped

2 scallions

2 tomatoes, chopped

Homemade Chimichurri Sauce

½ cup olive oil

1 teaspoon parsley

1 teaspoon red pepper flakes

2 garlic cloves

2 red onions

Directions:

— Season the washed and clean turkey with the salt, pepper, paprika and cayenne pepper.

— Rub it gently all over.

— Arrange the wood chip inside the smoker and then preheat the smoker to 230 degrees F.

— Transfer the turkey to the sheet pan and arrange peppers, onions, carrots, scallion, and tomatoes beside it.
— Drizzle the olive oil on top.
— Place the pan sheet inside the smoker.
— Close the electric smoker door and then cook for 4 hours at 250 degrees F.
— Check the turkey to an internal temperature of 165°F.
— Now, it is time to make the chimichurri.
— Blend all the homemade chimichurri ingredients in a blender and puree until combined.
— Serve the cooked turkey and veggie with the ready to serve the sauce.
— Enjoy!

Nutrition Facts per serving:

Calories 807 and Daily Value*
Total Fat 35.9g 46%
Saturated Fat 4.5g 23%
Cholesterol 283mg 94%
Sodium 920mg 40%
Total Carbohydrate 11.7g 4%
Dietary Fiber 2.9g 10%
Total Sugars 5.8g
Protein 94.8g
Calcium 32mg 2%
Iron 6mg 35%
Potassium 311mg 7%

Whole Smoked Turkey Recipe

Prep Time: 16 Hours • Cooking Time: 10 Hours • Servings: 14

Ingredients:

½ cup salt

⅓ cup molasses

⅓ cup granulated sugar

½ cup Worcestershire sauce

6 cloves, smashed garlic

4 dried bay leaves

Black pepper to taste

14 pounds whole turkey

2 cups bourbon

1 cup canola oil for coating

Directions:

— Pour a gallon of water, salt, sugar, molasses, garlic, Worcestershire sauce, bourbon, pepper, and bay leaves in a large pot.

— Boil it for a few minutes and then cool it down completely.

— Submerge the turkey completely in the brine using a large bucket.

— Brine it in the liquid for 15 hours.

— The next day, take the turkey out of the brine and pat dry with paper towel.

— Rub the turkey with oil and additional pepper.

— Load the smoker with soaked wood chips, and place the turkey inside the smoker for cooking.

— Set temperature to 250 degrees F.

— Once the internal temperate is 165 degrees F, the turkey is ready.

— Note: It took about 10 hours of cooking.

Nutrition Facts per serving:

Calories 770 and Daily Value*

Total Fat 29.2g 37%

Saturated Fat 1.7g 8%

Cholesterol 249mg 83%

Sodium 9583mg 417%

Total Carbohydrate 47.8g 17%

Dietary Fiber 1.9g 7%

Total Sugars 29g

Protein 61.3g

Calcium 95mg 7%

Iron 10mg 58%

Potassium 1705mg 36%

Classic Smoked Turkey Recipe

Prep Time: 30 Minutes • Cooking Time: 12 Hours • Servings: 16

Ingredients:

16 pounds turkey

2 tablespoons dried thyme

1 tablespoon dried sage

2 teaspoons dried oregano

2 teaspoons paprika

1 tablespoon sea salt

Black pepper, to taste

1 teaspoon dried rosemary

Zest of 1 orange

⅓ cup extra-virgin olive oil

⅓ cup apple cider

⅓ cups water

Directions:

— Preheat the electric smoker to 250 degrees F.

— Take a small bowl and mix all the dry spices and ingredients.

— Rub it gently over the rekey meat. At the end drizzle olive oil on top.

— Now pour water along with apple cider in the large water pan in the bottom of the electric smoker.

— Place a drip pan on the next rack or shelf of the smoker.

— Fill the sides with the apple wood chips.

— Place the turkey on the top rack of the smoker.

— Close the door of the rack and then cook for approximately 12 hours.

— Add more wood if smoke stops coming.

— Use the digital probe thermometer to get an internal temperature of 165 degrees F. Remove the turkey and serve.

Nutrition Facts per serving:

Calories 818 and Daily Value*

Total Fat 27g 35%

Saturated Fat 8.1g 41%

Cholesterol 343mg 114%

Sodium 669mg 29%

Total Carbohydrate 2.6g 1%

Dietary Fiber 0.7g 2%

Total Sugars 1.7g

Protein 133.1g

Calcium 31mg 2%

Iron 46mg 256%

Potassium 1393mg 30%

Turkey in the Electric Smoker

Prep Time: 1 Hour 10 Minutes • Cooking Time: 10 Hours • Servings: 10

Ingredients:

1 (10 pounds) whole turkey

4 cloves garlic, crushed

2 tablespoons salt, seasoned

½ cup butter

1 (12 fluid ounce) cola-flavored carbonated beverage

1 apple, quartered

1 onion, quartered

1 tablespoon garlic powder

1 tablespoon salt

1 tablespoon black pepper

Directions:

— Preheat your electric smoker to 225 degrees F and then rinse the turkey well under water, pat dry and then rub it with seasoned salt.

— Place it inside a roasting pan.

— Combine cola, butter, apples, garlic powder, salt, and pepper in a bowl .

— Fill the cavity of turkey with cola, apples, garlic powder, salt, and pepper.

— Rub butter and crushed garlic outside of the turkey as well.

— Cover the turkey with foil.

— Smoke the turkey for 10 hours at 250 degrees F.

— Once it's done, serve.

Nutrition Facts per serving:

Calories 907 and Daily Value*

Total Fat 63.2g 81%

Saturated Fat 22.3g 112%

Cholesterol 4256mg 1419%

Sodium 2364mg 103%

Total Carbohydrate 17.9g 6%

Dietary Fiber 1.1g 4%

Total Sugars 9.7g

Protein 62.7g

Calcium 462mg 36%

Iron 19mg 106%

Potassium 710mg 15%

chapter four
Seafood and Fish Recipes

Simple Salt & Pepper Smoked Salmon

Prep Time: 40 Minutes • Cooking Time: 2 Hours • Servings: 2

Ingredients:

2 pounds fresh salmon fillets
4 tablespoons melted butter
2 tablespoons lemon juice
Salt and pepper

Directions:

— Preheat the smoker to 225 degrees F. Add wood chips to begin the smoke.
— Now brush the butter over the fillets. Pour lemon juice over the fillets.
— Sprinkle the generous amount of pepper and salt to taste.
— Place salmon into the electric smoker. Cook for 2 hours.
— Once the fillets temperature reaches 150 degrees Fahrenheit, it's done.
— Serve and enjoy.

Nutrition Facts per serving:

Calories 807 and Daily Value*
Total Fat 51.2g 66%
Saturated Fat 18.7g 94%
Cholesterol 261mg 87%
Sodium 367mg 16%
Total Carbohydrate 0.4g 0%
Dietary Fiber 0.1g 0%
Total Sugars 0.3g
Protein 88.4g
Calcium 168mg 13%
Iron 3mg 16%
Potassium 1768mg 38%

Smoked Fish in a Brine

Prep Time: 12 Hours • Cooking Time: 5 Hours • Servings: 5

Ingredients:

5 pounds of fish fillets

BRINE Ingredients:

1 gallon water

cup brown sugar

2 cups canning salt

Directions:

— Combine sugar, water, and salt in a large pot.
— Split the fish into two halves and then soaks in the brine overnight.
— Prepare the electric smoker and then use apple wood chip to create smoke.
— Place the fish for cooking inside the smoker and let it cook for 5 hours at 225 F. The time depends on the temperature of how hot the smoker gets.

Nutrition Facts per serving:

Calories 773 and Daily Value*

Dietary Fiber 0g 0%

Total Fat 43.1g 55%

Total Sugars 18.8g

Saturated Fat 0g 0%

Protein 72.1g

Cholesterol 0mg 0%

Calcium 39mg 3%

Sodium 36892mg 1604%

Iron 0mg 1%

Total Carbohydrate 24.3g 9%

Potassium 33mg 1%

Classic Smoke Trout

Prep Time: 30 Minutes • Cooking Time: 4 Hours • Servings: 2

Ingredients for The Brine

3 cups water

1 cup of coarse salt

1-2 cups dark-brown sugar

Ingredients for The Trout

4 pounds of trout, backbone and pin bones removed

2 tablespoons vegetable oil for the grill basket

Directions:

— First, make the brine by mixing all the brine Ingredients: in a large pot.
— Submerge the fish in the brine for a few hours.
— Then pat dry the fish and drizzle oil all over the fish.
— Heat the smoker and add the wood chips.
— Fill the water pan with water. Wait until the smoke started to come out.
— Place a dripping pan beneath the grill grate to get all the drippings.
— Soak the wood in water and then add to coals.
— Smoke the fish for 4 hours at 225 degrees F, then serve.

Nutrition Facts per serving:

Calories 1400 and Daily Value*

Total Fat 52g 67%

Saturated Fat 9.4g 47%

Cholesterol 336mg 112%

Sodium 46425mg 2018%

Total Carbohydrate 107.9g 39%

Dietary Fiber 0g 0%

Total Sugars 106.7g

Protein 120.9g

Calcium 351mg 27%

Iron 9mg 53%

Potassium 2250mg 48%

Smoked Salmon

Prep Time: 2 Hours • Cooking Time: 5 Hours • Servings: 5

Ingredients:

5 pounds salmon, trout or char

1 ½ cup of maple syrup for basting

BRINE Ingredients:

1 quart cold water

⅓ cup Diamond Crystal kosher salt

1 cup brown sugar

Directions:

— Combine brine ingredients in a large bowl and place fish in for 2 hours. Next, pat dry the fish and let it dry. Place the fish on a rack and smoke the fish at 225 degrees F for 5 hours.

— After one hour of cooking, baste the chicken with the maple syrup repeat every one hour.

— The internal temperature of fish should be about 140°F to 150 degrees F.

— The smoked fish is ready to be served. Enjoy.

Nutrition Facts per serving:

Calories 725 and Daily Value*

Total Fat 10.7g 14%

Saturated Fat 2.2g 11%

Cholesterol 250mg 83%

Sodium 8141mg 354%

Total Carbohydrate 70.7g 26%

Dietary Fiber 0g 0%

Total Sugars 65.6g

Protein 89.3g

Calcium 107mg 8%

Iron 3mg 17%

Potassium 1816mg 39%

Smoked Fish with the Delicious Dip

Prep Time: 3 Hours • Cooking Time: 6 Hours • Servings: 6

Brine Ingredients:

1 quart cold water

⅓ cup salt

1 cup brown sugar

½ cup soy sauce

½ cup of vinegar

Ingredients for Sauce:

½ cup almond milk

6 ounces cream cheese, softened

⅓ cup finely minced onion

½ stalk celery, finely chopped

1 tablespoon minced fresh parsley

½ teaspoon lemon juice

1 teaspoon Worcestershire sauce

Cayenne pepper, to taste

Salt and black pepper to taste

Other Ingredients:

6 pounds of fish fillet

Directions:

— Combine the brine ingredients in a large bowl and place the fish in the brine for 2 hours.
— Next, blend all the sauce ingredients in a blender to make a smooth paste.
— Next, pat dries the fish with paper towel. Place the fish on a topmost rack of the smoker and smoke the fish at 225 degrees F for 6 hours.
— The internal temperature of fish should be about 150°F once done the cooking. Enjoy warm served with prepared sauce.

Nutrition Facts per serving:

Calories 1268 and Daily Value*
Total Fat 65.9g 84%
Saturated Fat 19g 95%
Cholesterol 185mg 62%
Sodium 10012mg 435%
Total Carbohydrate 104.8g 38%

Dietary Fiber 2.6g 9%
Total Sugars 24.9g
Protein 70.2g
Calcium 137mg 11%
Iron 11mg 59%
Potassium 1597mg 34%

Honey Mustard Halibut Fillets

Prep Time: 3 Hours • Cooking Time: 6 Hours • Servings: 6

Brine Ingredients:

⅓ cup kosher salt
1 cup brown sugar
4 tablespoons cumin

1 tablespoon dried bay leaves, crushed
½ gallon water

Other Ingredients:

6 halibut fillets
1 cup honey mustard rub

Directions:

— Combine and mix well all the brine ingredients in a large bowl and place the fish in it for 2 hours.
— Next, pat dry the fish and let it dry.
— Season the fish with the mustard rub and massage gently for fine coating.
— Place the fish on a rack inside the smoker and cook for 6 hours at 225 degrees F.
— The internal temperature of fish should be about 150°F at the end of cooking.
— Serve and enjoy.

Nutrition Facts per serving:

Calories 456 and Daily Value*

Total Fat 9.6g 12%

Saturated Fat 1.5g 8%

Cholesterol 101mg 4%

Sodium 6592mg 287%

Total Carbohydrate 27.1g 10%

Dietary Fiber 0.5g 2%

Total Sugars 23.8g

Protein 63.1g

Calcium 90mg 7%

Iron 16mg 90%

Potassium 1416mg 30%

Pineapple Maple Glaze Fish In the Smoker

Prep Time: 3 Hours • Cooking Time: 6 Hours • Servings: 6

Ingredients:

6 pounds fresh salmon

⅓ cup maple syrup

½ cup pineapple juice

Brine Ingredients:

½ gallon water

⅓ cup sea salt (non-iodized)

1 cup pineapple juice

¼ cup brown sugar

3 tablespoons Worcestershire sauce

2 tablespoons garlic salt

Directions:

— Prepare the brine by mixing all the brine ingredients in a large pot. Submerge the fish in it for 2 hours. Next, pat dry the fish and let it dry.
— Preheat the smoker to 225 degrees F.
— Place the dry salmon inside the smoker once the smoker starts to build.
— Place the fish in the smoker and cook it for 6 hours.
— Now mix ½ cup pineapple juice with maple syrup and baste the fish every 30 minutes, while cooking. Add soaked wood chip if the smoke is not enough.

Nutrition Facts per serving: 6

Calories 708 and Daily Value*

Total Fat 28.1g 36%

Saturated Fat 4g 20%

Cholesterol 200mg 67%

Sodium 5289mg 230%

Total Carbohydrate 26.6g 10%

Dietary Fiber 0.4g 1%

Total Sugars 22.6g

Protein 88.6g

Calcium 194mg 15%

Iron 3mg 19%

Potassium 1874mg 40%

Smoked Tuna

Prep Time: 12 Hours • Cooking Time: 90 Minutes • Servings: 2

Ingredients for The Tuna:

2 pounds tuna steaks

2 tablespoons soy sauce

Ingredients for The Brine:

6-10 cups warm water

½ cup salt

Dip Ingredients:

½ cup mayonnaise

2 ounces cream cheese

½ cup red onion, diced

⅓ cup fresh parsley, chopped

3 tablespoons lemon juice

½ tablespoon garlic powder

⅓ teaspoon black pepper

½ tablespoon hot sauce

Directions:

— Prepare brine by combining the entire brine ingredient in a pot.
— Soak the tuna in the brine overnight.
— Water should be enough to cover the tune well.
— Afterward, rinse under tap water.
— Pat dry the tuna with the paper towel, and then let it sit at room temperate to get dry.
— Rinse, dry, and lightly coat with soy sauce.
— Preheat the smoker and cook the tuna inside a smoker at 250 degrees F for 90 minutes.
— Meanwhile, prepare the sauce by mixing together the entire dip ingredient in a small bowl.
— Remove the tuna from smoker and let it get cold. Chop the tuna if desired.
— Add chopped tuna to the dip and let it sit in a refrigerator for a few minutes.
— Then serve.

Nutrition Facts per serving:

Calories 1200 and Daily Value*

Total Fat 58.3g 75%	Dietary Fiber 1.5g 5%
Saturated Fat 16.6g 3%	Total Sugars 6.4g
Cholesterol 269mg 90%	Protein 140.6g
Sodium 30031mg 1306%	Calcium 122mg 9%
Total Carbohydrate 21.6g 8%	Iron 8mg 43%
	Potassium 1703mg 36%

Smoked Eel

Prep Time: 12 Hours • Cooking Time: 3 Hours • Servings: 2

Ingredients for Brine:

10 cups warm water
1-½ cup salt
½ cup brown sugar

4 lemons, halved
2 sprigs fresh thyme

Other Ingredients:

2 fillets whole eel, cleaned and washed

Directions:

— First, prepare the brine by mixing all the brine ingredients in a large pot, and place eel in it for 10 hours. Next day, pat dry the eel and let it dry.
— Now, preheat the electric smoker to 235 degrees F and add wood chips.
— Smoke the eel for about 3 hours.
— Once the skins get crisp, the eel is ready to be served.
— Enjoy.

Nutrition Facts per serving:

Calories 549 and Daily Value*

Total Fat 24.2g 31%

Saturated Fat 4.9g 24%

Cholesterol 256mg 85%

Sodium 56739mg 2467%

Total Carbohydrate 47g 17%

Dietary Fiber 3.6g 13%

Total Sugars 38.1g

Protein 39g

Calcium 191mg 15%

Iron 4mg 21%

Potassium 795mg 17%

Smoked Catfish Recipe

Prep Time: 3 Hours • Cooking Time: 5 Hours • Servings: 5

Ingredients for The Rub:

3 tablespoons paprika

½ teaspoon salt

2 tablespoons garlic powder

2 tablespoons onion powder

⅓ tablespoon dried thyme

⅓ tablespoon cayenne

Other Ingredients:

5 fresh catfish fillets, about 1 pound each

4 tablespoons butter, soften

Directions:

— Mix all rub ingredients in a small bowl.
— Lightly rub the fillets with butter.
— Sprinkle the generous amount of rub onto fillets.
— Preheat the smoker to 225 degrees F,and add wood chips.
— Once the smoker starts to smoke, place the fish inside the smoker.
— Cook for 5 hours.
— Then serve.

Nutrition Facts per serving:

Calories 332 and Daily Value*
Total Fat 22g 28%
Saturated Fat 8.2g 41%
Cholesterol 100mg 33%
Sodium 387mg 17%
Total Carbohydrate 7.3g 3%
Dietary Fiber 2.2g 8%
Total Sugars 2.3g
Protein 26.5g
Calcium 41mg 3%
Iron 3mg 15%
Potassium 685mg 15%

chapter five

Vegetables & Side Dishes Recipes

Balsamic Glazed Potatoes and Carrots

Prep Time: 2 Hours • Cooking Time: 2 Hours • Servings: 3

Ingredients:

1 pound sweet potatoes

½ pound Yukon gold potatoes

4 ounces baby carrots

½ cup extra-virgin olive oil

Salt and pepper to taste

½ cup balsamic vinegar

Directions:

— Preheat the electric smoker to 225 degrees F by adding mild or any other wood chips.

— Peel, wash, and cut all the potatoes into 2-inch chunks.

— Combine potato chunks with baby carrot and then drizzle olive oil on the top.

— Season it with salt and pepper.

— Stir well to combine ingredients well.

— Place the ingredients in a large rack and smoker it for 1- 2 hours.

— Once potatoes are tender, drizzle balsamic vinegar on top.

— Enjoy.

Nutrition Facts per serving:

Calories 539 and Daily Value*

Total Fat 33.9g 43%

Saturated Fat 4.9g 24%

Cholesterol 0mg 0%

Sodium 45mg 2%

Total Carbohydrate 57.8g 21%

Dietary Fiber 9.3g 33%

Total Sugars 3.7g

Protein 3.6g

Calcium 41mg 3%

Iron 2mg 9%

Potassium 1665mg 35%

Smoked Corn

Prep Time: 2 hours 30 minutes • Cooking Time: 2-3 Hours • Servings: 8

Ingredients:

8 ears of corn

½ cup mayo

½ cup sour cream

1 handful fresh cilantro, chopped

2 teaspoons paprika

1 teaspoon cumin

Black pepper to taste

3 ounces spicy chipotle cream cheese, shredded

2 limes, sliced

Directions:

— Preheat the smoker to 225 degrees F for 2 hours.

— Next, husk the corn and remove the silk.

— Arrange the corn inside the smoker by tightly tying the husks together.

— Smoke for 2-3 hours. Combine the remaining listed ingredient in a small bowl. Serve it with smoked corn.

Nutrition Facts per serving:

Calories 261 and Daily Value*

Total Fat 12.7g 16%

Saturated Fat 4.7g 23%

Cholesterol 19mg 6%

Sodium 212mg 9%

Total Carbohydrate 36.3g 13%

Dietary Fiber 5g 18%

Total Sugars 7.1g

Protein 6.7g

Calcium 47mg 4%

Iron 5mg 25%

Potassium 505mg 11%

Smoked Green Beans

Prep Time: 50 Minutes • Cooking Time: 2 Hours • Servings: 3

Ingredients:

2.5 pounds fresh green beans
4 cups chicken broth or stock
1 pound smoked turkey legs meat

only
3 tablespoons apple cider vinegar
Salt and pepper, to taste

Directions:

— Add wood chips to the smoker and preheat the smoker for 40 minutes at 220 degrees F.
— Wash and then trim the edges of the green beans and place it in a microwave-safe container.
— Pour water over the beans and then microwave for 4 minutes.
— Drain the water.
— Pat dry the beans with the paper towel.
— Transfer the beans to a pan and cover with aluminum.
— Add stock and turkey to the same pan.
— Set the temperature of the smoker to 250 degrees F. Now cooks the green beans for 2 hours
— Once done, drain the excess liquid.
— Remove the turkey leg as well, and sprinkle the beans with the seasoning of salt, pepper, and a drizzle of apple cider vinegar and pepper.
— Serve with shredded turkey leg meat on top.

Nutrition Facts per serving:

Calories 390 and Daily Value*
Total Fat 8.8g 11%
Saturated Fat 2.8g 14%
Cholesterol 114mg 38%
Sodium 1148mg 50%
Total Carbohydrate 28.1g 10%

Dietary Fiber 12.9g 46%
Total Sugars 6.3g
Protein 52.1g
Calcium 165mg 13%
Iron 19mg 106%
Potassium 1271mg 27%

Lemon & Garlic Asparagus

Prep Time: 1 Hour • Cooking Time: 1.5 Hours • Servings: 1

Ingredients:

2 cups asparagus

Oil spray, for greasing

Salt and pepper, to taste

2 tablespoons butter

2 garlic cloves, minced

1 lemon

Directions:

— Prepare the electric smoker for 2 hours at 200 degrees F with a mild or any other wood chips.

— Trim and cut the asparagus into a 1-inch length.

— Put the asparagus in hot boiling water for one minute and then drain the water.

— Pat dry the vegetable with the paper towel.

— Toss the asparagus with the salt, pepper, and oil it with cooking spray.

— Set the temperature of the electric smoker to 250 degrees F and cooks the asparagus for 1.5 hours.

— Just before when the asparagus is ready to serve, melt the butter in a separate saucepan and add garlic.

— Do not fry the garlic.

— Once the asparagus is cooked to its perfection, transfer it to the serving tray and then top it off with butter dressing.

— Serve with the lemon squeeze on top.

Nutrition Facts per serving:

Calories 304 and Daily Value*

Total Fat 24.5g 31%

Saturated Fat 14.7g 74%

Cholesterol 61mg 20%

Sodium 170mg 7%

Total Carbohydrate 19.9g 7%

Dietary Fiber 9.3g 33%

Total Sugars 8.5g

Protein 8.8g

Calcium 87mg 7%

Iron 6mg 34%

Potassium 679mg 14%

Smoked Paprika Cauliflower

Prep Time: 40 Minutes • Cooking Time: 2 Hours • Servings: 2

Ingredients:

1 large head cauliflower, cut into florets

3 tablespoons olive oil

1 tablespoon white pepper

2 teaspoons smoked paprika

Directions:

— Preheat the electric smoker to 250 degrees with a mild or any other apple or cherry wood chips. Line a baking rack with the aluminum foil.

— Take a large mixing bowl and combine olive oil, smoked paprika and white pepper, and cauliflower

— Toss well.

— Smoke in electric smoke for 2 hours.

— Once it's done, serve.

Nutrition Facts per serving:

Calories 266 and Daily Value*

Total Fat 21.7g 28%

Saturated Fat 3.1g 16%

Cholesterol 0mg 0%

Sodium 88mg 4%

Total Carbohydrate 18.5g 7%

Dietary Fiber 8.8g 32%

Total Sugars 7.1g

Protein 6.4g

Calcium 81mg 6%

Iron 3mg 15%

Potassium 961mg 20

Side Dish Smoked Cabbage

Prep Time: 40 Minutes • Cooking Time: 2 Hours • Servings: 2

Ingredients:

2 large cups cabbage

3 tablespoons steak seasoning

1 stick butter

1 vegetable bouillon cube

Directions:

— Preheat the smoker, then add the hickory wood chips.
— Wash the cabbage well and then slice the cabbage.
— Put the cabbage into a tinfoil pan and place a stick of the butter on top.
— Then sprinkle the crushed vegetable bouillon cube.
— Sprinkle the steak seasoning at the end.
— Wrap it in the tin foil leaving a top slightly open.
— Once the smoke started to build, place the tin foil pan into the smoker and cook it for 2 hours at 250 degrees F. Once it's done, serve.

Nutrition Facts per serving:

Calories 427 and Daily Value*
Total Fat 46.1g 59%
Saturated Fat 29.1g 146%
Cholesterol 122mg 41%
Sodium 644mg 28%
Total Carbohydrate 4.5g 2%

Dietary Fiber 1.8g 6%
Total Sugars 2.6g
Protein 1.7g
Calcium 43mg 3%
Iron 0mg 2%
Potassium 141mg 3%

Eggplant in An Electric Smoker

Prep Time: 90 Minutes • Cooking Time: 1-2 Hours • Servings: 2

Ingredients:

3 cloves garlic, minced
4 tablespoons balsamic vinegar
Salt and pepper, to taste

4 eggplants
3 tablespoons olive oil

Directions:

— Preheat the smoke for 60 minutes by adding apple-flavor wood chips at 250 degrees F.
— Cut the eggplant into round, thick circles.
— Marinate the eggplant in a mixture of garlic, vinegar, salt, and pepper.

- Let it marinate for 30 minutes.
- Transfer the eggplant to the bowl and coat it with olive oil.
- Smoke inside the preheated electric smoker for 1-2 hours.
- Once it's done, serve.

Nutrition Facts per serving:

Calories 299 and Daily Value*

Total Fat 3.4g 4%

Saturated Fat 0.2g 1%

Cholesterol 0mg 0%

Sodium 24mg 1%

Total Carbohydrate 66.2g 24%

Dietary Fiber 38.8g 139%

Total Sugars 33.1g

Protein 11g

Calcium 109mg 8%

Iron 3mg 15%

Potassium 2550mg 54%

Potatoes Inside Smoker

Prep Time: 2 Hours 20 Minutes • Cooking Time: 2 Hours • Servings: 2

Ingredients:

⅓ cup olive oil

4 large potatoes

Salt and pepper, to taste

1 tablespoon onion powder

1 teaspoon garlic powder

1 teaspoon dried thyme

Directions:

- Preheat the electric smoker for two hours at 200 degrees by adding mild or any other wood chips.
- Cut the potatoes in half and then brush with the generous amount of olive oil.
- Now sprinkle salt, onion powder, garlic powder, dried thyme, and pepper on top.
- Smoke for 2 hours at 225 degrees F.
- Then, serve and enjoy.

Nutrition Facts per serving:

Calories 815 and Daily Value*

Total Fat 34.4g 44%

Saturated Fat 5g 25%

Cholesterol 0mg 0%

Sodium 47mg 2%

Total Carbohydrate 120.1g 44%

Dietary Fiber 18.3g 65%

Total Sugars 10.1g

Protein 13.1g

Calcium 90mg 7%

Iron 5mg 26%

Potassium 3056mg 65%

Zucchini & Squash

Prep Time: 2 Hours 10 Minutes • Cooking Time: 1 Hour • Servings: 3

Ingredients:

4 tablespoons balsamic vinegar

Salt and pepper, to taste

3 zucchinis

2 tablespoons vegetable oil

1 butternut squash

Directions:

— Preheat the electric smoker for two hours at 200 degrees by adding mild or any other wood chips.

— Slice the vegetables into ½ inch halves.

— Brush the vegetable with oil and sprinkle salt and pepper on top.

— Smoke it for 60 minutes at 250 degrees F.

— Once tender, take the vegetables out and drizzle vinegar on top.

Nutrition Facts per serving:

Calories 143 and Daily Value*

Total Fat 9.5g 12%

Saturated Fat 1.9g 9%

Cholesterol 0mg 0%

Sodium 23mg 1%

Total Carbohydrate 14g   5%

Dietary Fiber 4.4g   16%

Total Sugars 4.8g

Protein 3g

Calcium 34mg 3%

Iron 3mg 17%

Potassium 723mg   15%

Artichokes

Prep Time: 2 Hours 20 Minutes • Cooking Time: 2 Hours • Servings: 2

Ingredients:

2 artichokes

Dipping Sauce Ingredients:

½ cup melted butter

2 teaspoons dried thyme,

2 tablespoons fresh lemon juice

Salt and ground pepper, to taste

Directions:

— Preheat the electric smoker for one hour at 200 degrees F, by adding mild or any other wood chips.

— Trim the spikes from the artichokes and cut the base.

— Steam the artichoke for 20 minutes, then rinse off and pat dry with the paper towel. Once dry completely, smoke for 2 hours at 225 degrees F.

— Mix the entire dipping ingredient in a bowl and then serve it with smoked artichokes.

Nutrition Facts per serving:

Calories 489 and Daily Value*

Total Fat 46.5g 60%

Saturated Fat 29.4g 147%

Cholesterol 122mg 41%

Sodium 483mg 21%

Total Carbohydrate 18g 7%

Dietary Fiber 9.2g 33%

Total Sugars 2g

Protein 6g

Calcium 105mg 8%

Iron 3mg 18%

Potassium 640mg 14%

Mix Vegetables

Prep Time: 30 Minutes • Cooking Time: 2 Hours • Servings: 2

Ingredients:

2 ears fresh corn, husks and silk strands removed, cut into small pieces

2 yellow squash, cut into ½-inch thick slices

2 red onions, cubed

3 green bell peppers, cut into strips

1 yellow bell pepper, cut into strips

2 cups mushrooms, halved

2 tablespoons cooking oil, vegetable

2 tablespoons chicken seasoning

Directions:

— Preheat the electric smoker to 200 degrees F with a mild or any other wood chips.

— Toss all the listed ingredients together, and transfer it to the grill basket.

— Smoke it for about 2 hours at 225 F. Once it's done, serve as a side dish.

Nutrition Facts per serving:

Calories 425 and Daily Value*

Total Fat 16.7g 21%

Saturated Fat 2.4g 12%

Cholesterol 0mg 0%

Sodium 83mg 4%

Total Carbohydrate 67.5g 25%

Dietary Fiber 12.7g 45%

Total Sugars 23.3g

Protein 13.5g

Calcium 80mg 6%

Iron 8mg 45%

Potassium 1846mg 39%

Bacon Wrapped Mushrooms

Prep Time: 2 Hours • Cooking Time: 90 Minutes • Servings: 4

Ingredients:

12 white mushrooms

12 bacon strips, slices thin, center-cut bacon

1 tablespoon olive oil

2 garlic cloves, chopped
Salt and pepper to taste

1-2 sliced jalapeno pepper
½ cup of hot sauce (optional)

Directions:

— Preheat the smoker to 225 degrees F by adding apple wood chips and wait until smoke starts to come out.

— Brush each mushroom with olive oil and then place sliced jalapeño ring on a cap of a mushroom. Insert garlic pieces into the cavity of mushroom.

— Wrap each mushroom with one bacon strip.

— Twist the end of the bacon strips and let it drape down the sides of the mushrooms.

— Place these stuffed mushrooms filling side up, onto a baking rack and smoke for 90 minutes.

— Sprinkle salt and pepper at the end and then serve with hot sauce.

Nutrition Facts per serving:

Calories 355 and Daily Value*
Total Fat 31.5g 40%
Saturated Fat 9.7g 48%
Cholesterol 3mg 1%
Sodium 1707mg 74%
Total Carbohydrate 2.5g 1%

Dietary Fiber 0.7g 3%
Total Sugars 1.5g
Protein 14.4g
Calcium 4mg 0%
Iron 2mg 10%
Potassium 228mg 5%

Smoked Brussels Sprouts

Prep Time: 2 Hours • Cooking Time: 90 Minutes • Servings: 2

Ingredients:

1.5 pounds of Brussels sprouts
6 tablespoons olive oil
2 tablespoons Dijon mustard
6 cloves garlic, minced
2 sprig thyme

½ teaspoon smoked paprika
2 teaspoons apple cider vinegar
½ teaspoon fresh-cracked pepper
¼ teaspoon kosher salt

Directions:

— Preheat the electric smoker for two hours at 200 degrees F by adding a mild or any other wood chips.
— Chop the Brussels sprouts in a large bowl.
— Add in all the listed ingredients and toss well for fine coating.
— Place the Brussels sprouts in a non-stick rack and place inside the smoker.
— Cook for 90 minutes at 220 degrees F.
— Enjoy.

Nutrition Facts per serving:

Calories 534 and Daily Value*

Total Fat 43.9g 56%

Saturated Fat 6.5g 32%

Cholesterol 0mg 0%

Sodium 458mg 20%

Total Carbohydrate 35.2g 13%

Dietary Fiber 13.7g 49%

Total Sugars 7.6g

Protein 13g

Calcium 144mg 11%

Iron 5mg 27%

Potassium 1398mg 30%

Mixed Smoked Vegetables

Prep Time: 2 Hours 10 Minutes • Cooking Time: 60-80 Minutes • Servings: 4

Ingredients:

4 large carrots cut into cubes

2 russet potatoes, unpeeled and cut into small chunks

4 sweet potatoes, cut into chunks

½ cup extra-virgin olive oil

Ground black pepper, to taste

Sea salt, to taste

2 tablespoons parsley

Directions:

— Preheat the electric smoker for two at 200 degrees F by adding in the mild or any other wood chips.
— Toss all the vegetables with the listed ingredients in a large bowl.
— Mix well with a fine coating.

— Place the vegetable in the aluminum foil pan.
— Place the pan into the preheated smoker and cook for 60- 80 minutes at 220 degrees F.
— Once the vegetables get tender, transfer to serving plate and drizzle a bit more olive oil on top.
— Season as desired and serve.

Nutrition Facts per serving:

Calories 408 and Daily Value*
Total Fat 25.5g 33%
Saturated Fat 3.7g 18%
Cholesterol 0mg 0%
Sodium 122mg 5%
Total Carbohydrate 44.9g 16%

Dietary Fiber 7.5g 27%
Total Sugars 5.2g
Protein 3.6g
Calcium 49mg 4%
Iron 1mg 7%
Potassium 1287mg 27%

Smoked Vegetables

Prep Time: 1 Hour • Cooking Time: 2 Hours • Servings: 2

Ingredients:

4 zucchinis, cut into slices
12 green onions
2 red bell peppers, sliced

4 tablespoons olive oil
Sea salt, to taste
Black pepper, to taste

Directions:

— Preheat the smoker to 225 degrees F and add apple wood chips.
— Now take a bowl and mix all the ingredients well.
— Coat well the vegetables.
— Transfer to the skillet.
— Place in preheat smoker and let it cook for 2 hours.
— Serve warm or at room temperature.

Nutrition Facts per serving:

Calories 370 and Daily Value*

Total Fat 29.2g 37%

Saturated Fat 4.2g 21%

Cholesterol 0mg 0%

Sodium 174mg 8%

Total Carbohydrate 28.8g 10%

Dietary Fiber 8.3g 30%

Total Sugars 14.9g

Protein 7.6g

Calcium 134mg 10%

Iron 3mg 18%

Potassium 1500mg 32%

Grilled Pumpkin With Cinnamon Whiskey Glaze

Prep Time: 25 Minutes • Cooking Time: 2-3 Hours • Servings: 2

Ingredients:

1 large pie pumpkin

Oil spray, for greasing

Seasoning Ingredients:

2 tablespoons light brown sugar

2 teaspoons ground cinnamon

½ teaspoon grated nutmeg

½ teaspoon ground ginger,

½ teaspoon orange zest, dried

¼ teaspoon ground allspice

For The Glaze Ingredients:

1 cup chicken stock

¼ cup light brown sugar

2 tablespoons cornstarch

2 tablespoons cold water

4 ounces cinnamon whiskey

Directions:

— Take a small cooking pot and pour stock in it

— Bring it to medium heat and cook for 10 minutes.

— Once reduced to half add brown sugar and stir well until combined.

— Add in the cornstarch and water together and cook for 2 minutes, while stirring the liquid.

- Next, add cinnamon whiskey and stir to combine well.
- Turn off the heat.
- Wash and clean the pumpkin and cut into slices with the knife.
- Take out the seeds and clean the inside of it.
- Cut into cubes.
- Spray the pumpkin slices with oil, then sprinkles the pumpkin with the seasoning ingredients.
- Cover the pumpkin with glaze mixture and place in the smoker and let it cool for 2-3 hours at 225 degrees F.
- Serve warm.

Nutrition Facts per serving:

Calories 162 and Daily Value*
Total Fat 5.7g 7%
Saturated Fat 1.2g 6%
Cholesterol 11mg 4%
Sodium 157mg 7%
Total Carbohydrate 26.4g 10%

Dietary Fiber 2.9g 11%
Total Sugars 16.5g
Protein 2.3g
Calcium 67mg 5%
Iron 1mg 4%
Potassium 117mg 2%

Smoked Sweet Mushroom

Prep Time: 10 Minutes • Cooking Time: 45 Minutes • Servings: 1

Ingredients:

1 tablespoon onion powder
1 teaspoon sugar
Salt, to taste

Pepper to taste
4 cups mushroom
1 tablespoon canola oil

Directions:

- Wash and clean the mushroom and pat dry with paper towel.
- Preheat the smoker to 350 degrees F by adding apple wood chips.
- Combine mushroom along with all the listed ingredients in a bowl.

— Transfer the mushroom to rack and place inside the smoker for cooking.
— Cook for 30 minutes and then turn the temperature to 450 degrees F and smoker for additional 15 minutes.
— Serve.

Nutrition Facts per serving:

Calories 223 and Daily Value*

Total Fat 14.9g 19%

Saturated Fat 1g 5%

Cholesterol 0mg 0%

Sodium 175mg 8%

Total Carbohydrate 18.8g 7%

Dietary Fiber 3.2g 12%

Total Sugars 11.3g

Protein 9.5g

Calcium 26mg 2%

Iron 8mg 46%

Potassium 957mg 20%

Potato Torte Inside A Smoker

Prep Time: 1 Hour • Cooking Time: 90 Minutes • Servings: 6

Ingredients:

6 potatoes, scrubbed but not skinned

3 tablespoons olive oil

Salt and black pepper to taste

3 tablespoons fresh rosemary, chopped

Directions:

— Preheat the smoker at 220 degrees F for 40 minutes by adding a wood chip of apple flavor.
— Sprayed a heavy skillet with oiland then set aside for further use.
— Take a mandolin and thinly slice the potatoes.
— Place the potatoes in the skillet. As you add the slices, brush the potatoes with olive oil and sprinkle salt and pepper along with the rosemary.
— Cook inside the smoker until start to sizzle for about an hour.
— Carefully invert the torte on a flat plate.
— Return the torte to the cooking skillet and place in the smoker for additional cooking for 30 minutes. Then serve.

Nutrition Facts per serving:

Calories 212 and Daily Value*

Total Fat 7.5g 10%

Saturated Fat 1.2g 6%

Cholesterol 0mg 0%

Sodium 14mg 1%

Total Carbohydrate 34.5g 13%

Dietary Fiber 5.8g 21%

Total Sugars 2.5g

Protein 3.7g

Calcium 40mg 3%

Iron 2mg 9%

Potassium 883mg 19%

Smoked Onions With Cheese

Prep Time: 50 Minutes • Cooking Time: 45 Minutes • Servings: 3

Ingredients:

6 slices whole grain bread

6 tablespoons butter (more or less) at room temperature

6 slices good cheddar cheese

2 sweet onion, sliced thinly

6 thin slices prosciutto

Directions:

— Preheat the smoker for 30 minutes at 350 degrees F.

— Place onions inside the smoker and let it cook for 45 minutes.

— Take out the onions and then slice thinly.

— Place butter on each slice of bread and top three bread slices with one slice of cheese, generous amount of onion, one slice of prosciutto and one slice of cheddar cheese.

— Place remaining slices on the top of the cheddar cheese.

— Assemble all slices in the form of a sandwich.

— Serve and enjoy.

Nutrition Facts per serving:

Calories 729 and Daily Value*

Total Fat 48.9g 63%

Saturated Fat 15g 75%

Cholesterol 57mg 19%

Sodium 1177mg 51%

Total Carbohydrate 46.5g 17%

Dietary Fiber 9.4g 34%
Total Sugars 13.8g
Protein 36.8g

Calcium 636mg 49%
Iron 8mg 44%
Potassium 522mg 11%

Smoked Tomatoes

Prep Time: 30 Minutes • Cooking Time: 60 Minutes • Servings: 2

Ingredients:

10 plum tomatoes
Salt and pepper, to taste

Thyme to taste

Directions:

— Preheat the smoker to 225 degrees F by adding hickory smoker chips.
— Remember to soak the wood chips in water for 60 minutes before adding to the smoker. Season the tomatoes with listed ingredients.
— Layer the tomatoes on a rack or baking pan and then cook inside the smoker for 60 minutes. Serve as a side dish.

Nutrition Facts per serving:

Calories 142 and Daily Value*
Total Fat 1.2g 2%
Saturated Fat 0.2g 1%
Cholesterol 0mg 0%
Sodium 80mg 3%
Total Carbohydrate 31.4g 11%
Dietary Fiber 6.8g 24%
Total Sugars 24.6g
Protein 7.4g
Calcium 81mg 6%
Iron 3mg 18%
Potassium 1256mg 27%

chapter six
Desserts Recipes

Blueberry Crumble

Prep Time: 50 Minutes • Cooking Time: 3.5 Hours • Servings: 4

Filling Ingredients:

1 cup blueberries

¾ cup dark brown sugar

½ cup self-rising flour

2 teaspoons lemon zest, grated

2 tablespoons lemon juice

Ingredients for Crumble:

1.5 cups quick-cooking oats

⅓ cup all-purpose flour

½ cup packed brown sugar

2 teaspoons cinnamon

⅓ cup butter

Directions:

— Place the washed the blueberries in a mixing bowl and add sugar, lemon zest, lemon juice, and flour.

— Mix all the ingredients well.

— Take an aluminum pan and coat it with oil spray.

— Spoon the filling into the pan.

— Then combine all the crumble ingredients in a separate bowl and pour over the blueberry mixture in the pan.

— Cook in the electric smoker for 3.5 hours at 260 degrees F.

— Once done, serve.

Nutrition Facts per serving:

Calories 531 and Daily Value*

Total Fat 17.7g 23%

Saturated Fat 10.1g 51%

Cholesterol 41mg 14%

Sodium 216mg 9%

Total Carbohydrate 90.3g 33%

Dietary Fiber 5.2g 19%

Total Sugars 39.4g

Protein 5.3g

Calcium 71mg 5%

Iron 2mg 13%

Potassium 209mg 4%

Baked Peach Cobbler

Prep Time: 50 Minutes • Cooking Time: 3 Hours • Servings: 4

Ingredients:

2 teaspoons melted butter

3 pounds sliced peaches

½ cup maple syrup

1 cup self-rising flour

3/4 tsp baking powder

1 pinch cinnamon

1 pinch salt

⅓ cup unsalted butter, cut into small cubes

⅓ cup white sugar

2 eggs

½ tsp vanilla

Directions:

— Set the electric smoker temperature to 220 degrees F, and add cherry wood chips.

— Coat a large heatproof pan with melted butter.

— Take a bowl and toss peaches with maple syrup.

— In a small bowl, combine flour, baking powder, salt and cinnamon, and set it aside.

— In a separate bowl, mix butter along with sugar.

— Then add eggs and the vanilla extract.

— Combine the flour mixture with egg mixture.

— Spoon this batter on top of peaches.

— Cook in the electric smoker for 3 hours at 260 degrees F. Once done serve.

Nutrition Facts per serving:

Calories 510 and Daily Value*
Total Fat 20.1g 26%
Saturated Fat 11.7g 58%
Cholesterol 128mg 43%
Sodium 90mg 4%
Total Carbohydrate 78.2g 28%

Dietary Fiber 2.6g 9%
Total Sugars 50.9g
Protein 7.2g
Calcium 89mg 7%
Iron 3mg 15%
Potassium 458mg 10%

Rhubarb Cobbler

Prep Time: 1 Hour • Cooking Time: 3 Hours • Servings: 3

Ingredients:

1 pound rhubarb, chopped
⅓ cup brown sugar
Pinch of salt

1 teaspoon lemon juice
1 tablespoon lemon zest
2 teaspoons vanilla extract

Cobbler Topping Ingredients:

1.5 cups all-purpose flour
4 tablespoons sugar
1 teaspoon baking powder

¼ tsp kosher salt
10 tablespoons unsalted butter
⅓ cup sour cream

Directions:

— Start the electric smoker and add mild flavor wood chips and wait until the smoke is established.
— Set temperature to 260 degrees F.
— Take a medium bowl and mix cobbler topping ingredients including salt, flour, baking powder, and sugar
— Add butter and sour cream.
— Mix gently with the fork to form the smooth dough.
— Take a small bowl and then mix chopped rhubarb, lemon juice, lemon zest, vanilla extract, and salt, and sugar.

— Transfer this mixture to the desired baking dish.
— Spoon the prepared dough on top.
— Place it inside smoker and cooks for 3hours or until the top gets brown and bubbling.
— Serve.

Nutrition Facts per serving:

Calories   638 and Daily Value*

Total Fat 27.9g 36%

Saturated Fat 17.2g 86%

Cholesterol 69mg   23%

Sodium 232mg 10%

Total Carbohydrate 89g   32%

Dietary Fiber 4.6g   16%

Total Sugars 34g

Protein 8.9g

Calcium 263mg   20%

Iron 4mg   20%

Potassium 748mg   16%

Chocolate Cobbler

Prep Time: 50 Minutes • Cooking Time: 80 Minutes • Servings: 3

Ingredients:

2 cups chocolate, chopped

1 cup whipped cream, (for a topping)

Cobbler Topping Ingredients:

1.5 cups all-purpose flour

4 tablespoons sugar

1 teaspoon baking powder

5 tablespoons cocoa powder

½ cup sour cream

Directions:

— Start the smoker and add wood chips and wait until the smoke is established.
— Set temperature to 350 degrees F.
— Meanwhile, take a separate medium bowl and mix together the sugar, flour, baking soda, and cocoa powder.
— Add the sour cream.
— Mix gently to form a dough.

— Add chocolate pieces to a baking bowl and pour the dough mixture on top.
— Place it inside smoker and cooks or 80 minutes or until top get brown and bubbling.
— Serve with whipped cream if desired.

Nutrition Facts per serving:

Calories 1107 and Daily Value*
Total Fat 55.4g 71%
Saturated Fat 36.8g184%
Cholesterol 87mg   29%
Sodium 127mg 6%
Total Carbohydrate 138.8g 50%

Dietary Fiber 8.2g   29%
Total Sugars 74.1g
Protein 18.7g
Calcium 375mg 29%
Iron 7mg 39%
Potassium 972mg 21%

Cherry Crumble

Prep Time: 50 Minutes • Cooking Time: 3 Hours • Servings: 4

Ingredients:

Filling Ingredients:

1 cup of cherries
¾ cup dark brown sugar

1 cup self-rising flour

Ingredients for Crumble:

1.5 cup quick oats
⅓ cup all-purpose flour

½ cup raisin
⅓ cup butter

Directions:

— Place the washed cherries in a mixing bowl and add sugar and flour, and mix gently.
— Take the aluminum pan and coat it with oil spray.
— Spoon the flour filling into the aluminum pan.
— Add oats, raisins, butter, and flour.

- Mix well until it is lumpy in consistency.
- Cook in an electric smoker or 3 hours at 260 degrees F.
- Once it's done, serve.

Nutrition Facts per serving:

Calories 654 and Daily Value*

Total Fat 17.7g 23%

Saturated Fat 10.1g 50%

Cholesterol 41mg 14%

Sodium 306mg 13%

Total Carbohydrate 120.2g 44%

Dietary Fiber 5.5g 20%

Total Sugars 42.3g

Protein 6.3g

Calcium 72mg 6%

Iron 2mg 11%

Potassium 368mg 8%

chapter seven
Sauce and Rubs Recipes

Simple Smoked Salt Recipe

Prep Time: 30 Minutes • Cooking Time: 60 Minutes • Servings: 2

Ingredients:

½ cup kosher salt

Directions:

— Preheat the eclectic smoke to 220 degrees F.

— Use a cold smoker attachment and fired up the apple wood chips until the temperature reaches 100 degrees F.

— Next, take an aluminum pie pan and place about ½ cup of kosher salt into it.

— Place in the smoker to start the smoking process.

— After an hour the salt is smoked to its perfection.

— Store it in a tight jar for future use.

Nutrition Facts per serving:

Calories 0 and Daily Value*

Total Fat 0g 0%

Saturated Fat 0g 0%

Cholesterol 0mg 0%

Sodium 28293mg 1230%

Total Carbohydrate 0g 0%

Dietary Fiber 0g 0%

Total Sugars 0g

Protein 0g

Calcium 18mg 1%

Iron 0mg 1%

Potassium 6mg 0%

Chicken Spice Rub

Prep Time: 50 Minutes • Cooking Time: 1-2 Hours • Servings: 2

Ingredients:

1 teaspoon sea salt

4 teaspoons dried basil

4 teaspoons crushed dried rosemary

2 teaspoons garlic powder

4 teaspoons dry mustard powder

1 teaspoon paprika

¼ teaspoon ground black pepper

¼ teaspoon ground dried thyme

½ teaspoon celery seed

1 teaspoon dried parsley

½ teaspoon ground cumin

½ teaspoon cayenne pepper

Directions:

— Combine all the spice in a large bowl. Preheat the electric smoke to 220 degrees F. Use a cold smoker attachment and fired up the apple wood chips until the temperature reaches 100 degrees F.

— Take an aluminum pie pan and place bowl spices into it.

— Place inside the smoker and close the door. After 1-2 hours the spices are smoked to perfection. Store it in a tight jar for future use.

Nutrition Facts per serving:

Calories 60 and Daily Value*

Total Fat 2.8g 4%

Saturated Fat 0.3g 2%

Cholesterol 0mg 0%

Sodium 941mg 41%

Total Carbohydrate 7.5g 3%

Dietary Fiber 3g 11%

Total Sugars 1.3g

Protein 2.7g

Calcium 89mg 7%

Iron 2mg 14%

Potassium 161mg 3%

Zest Herbal Rub

Prep Time: 60 Minutes • Cooking Time: 60 -120 Minutes • Servings: 3

Ingredients:

½ cup cane sugar

⅓ cup chili powder

2 tablespoons granulated onion

2 tablespoons granulated garlic

1 tablespoon dried chilies

1 tablespoon dill weed

3 tablespoons lemon powder

2 tablespoons cumin, ground

2 tablespoons celery seeds

2 tablespoons basil

½ tablespoon dried rosemary

½ tablespoon mustard powder

Directions:

— Combine all the spice in a bowl.

— Preheat the eclectic smoke to 220 degrees F.

— Use a cold smoker attachment and fire up the apple wood chips until the temperature reaches 100 degrees F.

— Next, take an aluminum pie pan and place bowl spices into it.

— Place the pan inside the smoker and let it smoke for 1 or 2 hours.

— After an hour, the spices are smoked to perfection.

— Store it in the tight jar for future use.

Nutrition Facts per serving:

Calories 279 and Daily Value*

Total Fat 5.2g 7%

Saturated Fat 0.7g 3%

Cholesterol 0mg 0%

Sodium 1549mg 67%

Total Carbohydrate 58.2g 21%

Dietary Fiber 7.9g 28%

Total Sugars 32g

Protein 6.4g

Calcium 220mg 17%

Iron 8mg 44%

Potassium 2127mg 45%

BBQ Rub

Prep Time: 60 Minutes • Cooking Time: 60-120 Minutes • Servings: 2

Ingredients:

½ cup brown sugar

½ cup paprika

1 tablespoon ground black pepper

½ tablespoon salt

3 tablespoons chili powder

4 tablespoons garlic powder

4 tablespoons onion powder

1 teaspoon cayenne pepper

Directions:

— Combine all the spice in a bowl. Preheat the electric smoke to 220 F.

— Use a cold smoker attachment and fire up the apple wood chips until the temperature reaches 100 degrees F.

— Next, take an aluminum pie pan and place the spices from the bowl into it.

— Place the pan inside the smoker and let it smoke for 1 to 2 hours.

— Store it in the tight jar for future use.

Nutrition Facts per serving:

Calories 361 and Daily Value*

Total Fat 5.7g 7%

Saturated Fat 1g 5%

Cholesterol 0mg 0%

Sodium 1890mg 82%

Total Carbohydrate 81.7g 30%

Dietary Fiber 16.8g 60%

Total Sugars 47.7g

Protein 9.8g

Calcium 186mg 14%

Iron 10mg 53%

Potassium 1228mg 26%

Magical Rub Mix

Prep Time: 60 Minutes • Cooking Time: 120 Minutes • Servings: 3

Ingredients:

½ cup paprika

½ teaspoon brown sugar

2 tablespoons salt

4 tablespoons white pepper

4 tablespoons mustard

Directions:

— Combine all the spice in a bowl.
— Preheat the smoke to 220 degrees F.
— Use a cold smoker attachment and fire up the apple wood chips until the temperature reaches 100 degrees F.
— Next, take an aluminum pie pan and place bowl spices into it.
— Place the pan inside the smoker and let it smoke for 2 hours.
— After an hour, the spices are smoked to perfection.
— Store it in the tight jar for future use.

Nutrition Facts per serving:

Calories 280 and Daily Value*
Total Fat 6.8g 9%
Saturated Fat 0.7g 3%
Cholesterol 0mg 0%
Sodium 4671mg 203%
Total Carbohydrate 56.1g 20%

Dietary Fiber 10.7g 38%
Total Sugars 38.4g
Protein 7.2g
Calcium 178mg 14%
Iron 8mg 46%
Potassium 653mg 14%

Cajun Spice Rub

Prep Time: 60 Minutes • Cooking Time: 60 Minutes • Servings: 4

Ingredients:

½ tablespoon salt
4 teaspoons ground cayenne pepper
3 teaspoons ground white pepper
4 teaspoons ground black pepper

4 teaspoons paprika
4 teaspoons onion powder
3 teaspoons garlic powder

Directions:

— Combine all the spice in a bowl.
— Preheat the smoke to 220 degrees F.
— Use a cold smoker attachment and fire up the apple wood chips until the temperature reaches 100 degrees F.

- Next, take an aluminum pie pan and place bowl spices into it.
- Place the pan inside the smoker and let it smoke for one hour.
- After an hour, the spices are smoked to perfection.
- Store spices in a tight jar for future use.

Nutrition Facts per serving:

Calories 32 and Daily Value*

Total Fat 0.7g 1%

Saturated Fat 0.1g 1%

Cholesterol 0mg 0%

Sodium 876mg 38%

Total Carbohydrate 7g 3%

Dietary Fiber 2.2g 8%

Total Sugars 1.8g

Protein 1.4g

Calcium 26mg 2%

Iron 1mg 8%

Potassium 158mg 3%

Queens of Cuisine Seafood Seasoning

Prep Time: 60 Minutes • Cooking Time: 120 Minutes • Servings: 4

Ingredients:

2 teaspoons paprika

4 teaspoons cinnamon

3 teaspoons ground ginger

2 teaspoons ground cumin

2 teaspoons ground coriander

2 teaspoons dried lemon peel

4 teaspoons onion powder

2 teaspoons lemon pepper

2 teaspoons dried parsley

2 teaspoons dried cilantro

2 teaspoons garlic powder

Directions:

- Combine all the spice in a bowl.
- Preheat the electric smoke to 220 degrees F.
- Use a cold smoker attachment and fire up with the cherry wood chips until the temperature reaches 100 degrees F.
- Next, take an aluminum pie pan and place bowl spices into it.
- Place the pan inside the smoker and let it smoke for 2 hours.
- After 2 hours, the spices are smoked to perfection. Store in the tight jar for future use.

Nutrition Facts per serving:

Calories 34 and Daily Value*

Total Fat 0.6g 1%

Saturated Fat 0.1g 0%

Cholesterol 0 mg 0%

Sodium 5mg 0%

Total Carbohydrate 7.8g 3%

Dietary Fiber 2.5g 9%

Total Sugars 1.5g

Protein 1.2g

Calcium 52mg 4%

Iron 2mg 10%

Potassium 130mg 3%

Three Pepper Rub

Prep Time: 60 Minutes • Cooking Time: 2 Hours • Servings: 4

Yield: 1 Cup Ingredients

4 tablespoons black pepper

4 tablespoons white pepper

1 tablespoon red pepper

2 tablespoons onion powder

2 teaspoons garlic powder

1 tablespoon dried thyme

2 tablespoons paprika

4 tablespoons dried oregano

Directions:

— Combine all the spice in a bowl.

— Preheat the smoke to 220 degrees F.

— Use a cold smoker attachment and fire up the hickory wood chips until the temperature reaches 100 degrees F.

— Next, take an aluminum pie pan and place bowl spices into it.

— Place the pan inside the smoker and let it smoke for 2 hours.

— After 3 hours, the spices are smoked to perfection.

— Store it in the tight jar for future use.

Nutrition Facts per serving:

Calories 89 and Daily Value*

Total Fat 1.5g 2%

Saturated Fat 0.3g 2%

Cholesterol 0mg 0%

Sodium 8mg 0%

Total Carbohydrate 20.3g 7%

Dietary Fiber 7.8g 28%

Total Sugars 3.7g

Protein 3.4g

Calcium 153mg 12%

Iron 7mg 38%

Potassium 351mg 7%

Jerky Seasoning

Prep Time: 60 Minutes • Cooking Time: 2 Hours • Servings: 1

Ingredients:

6 tablespoons dried minced onion

4 teaspoons dried thyme

2 teaspoons ground allspice powder

1 teaspoon ground black pepper

2 teaspoons ground cinnamon

2 teaspoons cayenne pepper

Directions:

— Combine all the spice in a bowl.

— Preheat the smoke to 220 degrees F.

— Use a cold smoker attachment and fire up the apple flavored wood chips until the temperature reached 100 degrees F.

— Next, take an aluminum pie pan and place bowl spices into it.

— Place the pan inside the smoker and let it smoke for 2 hours.

— Store spices in a tight jar for future use.

Nutrition Facts per serving:

Calories 73 and Daily Value*

Total Fat 1.4g 2%

Saturated Fat 0.4g 2%

Cholesterol 0mg 0%

Sodium 2335mg 102%

Total Carbohydrate 18g 7%

Dietary Fiber 7.6g 27%

Total Sugars 3.1g

Protein 2.1g

Calcium 177mg 14%

Iron 7mg 37%

Potassium 279mg 6%

Classic Rub Recipes

Prep Time: 60 Minutes • Cooking Time: 2 Hours • Servings: 1

Ingredients:

4 tablespoons brown sugar

1 tablespoon paprika

2 tablespoons salt

1 tablespoon ground black pepper

2 teaspoons garlic powder

Directions:

— Combine all the spice in a bowl.

— Preheat the smoker to 220 degrees F.

— Use a cold smoker attachment and fire up the mildly flavored wood chips until the temperature reaches 100 degrees F.

— Next, take an aluminum pie pan and place bowl spices into it.

— Place the pan inside the smoker and let it smoke for 2 hours.

— After 2 hours, the spices are smoked to perfection.

— Store it in a tight jar for future use.

Nutrition Facts per serving:

Calories 192 and Daily Value*

Total Fat 1.1g 1%

Saturated Fat 0.2g 1%

Cholesterol 0mg 0%

Sodium 13970mg 607%

Total Carbohydrate 47.4g 17%

Dietary Fiber 4.8g 17%

Total Sugars 37g

Protein 2.7g

Calcium 83mg 6%

Iron 4mg 22%

Potassium 355mg 8%

chapter eigth
Meat Recipes

Honey Balsamic Glazed Lamb Chops

Prep Time: 1 Hour • Cooking Time: 3 Hours • Servings: 4

Ingredients for The Dry Spices

½ teaspoon salt
½ teaspoon paprika
¼ teaspoon garlic powder

1 teaspoon dried mustard
½ teaspoon thyme

Other Ingredients:

12 lamb chops
4 teaspoons honey

2 teaspoons balsamic vinegar

Directions:

— Cut the lamb into pieces with a sharp knife.
— Mix all dry spices together in a large bowl.
— Rub the spices on the lamb and massage for fine coating.
— Place the lamb in a zip-lock plastic bag and then marinate in the refrigerator for an hour.
— Grease skillet with oil spray and then add the marinated lamb in it.
— Cook in the smoker at 220 degrees F for 3 hours.
— Drizzle some honey and vinegar at the very end after taking out the lamb for a little sweetness.
— Enjoy.

Nutrition Facts per serving:

Calories 801 and Daily Value*

Total Fat 64.2g 82%

Saturated Fat 30g 150%

Cholesterol 0mg 0%

Sodium 471mg 20%

Total Carbohydrate 6.4g   2%

Dietary Fiber 0.3g   1%

Total Sugars 5.9g

Protein 50.4g

Calcium 8mg 1%

Iron 0mg 2%

Potassium 20mg 0%

Rack of Lamb

Prep Time: 1 Hour • Cooking Time: 3 Hours • Servings: 3

Ingredients:

Spices

½ teaspoon garlic powder

1 teaspoon onion powder

2 teaspoons thyme

2 teaspoons basil

2 teaspoons salt

½ teaspoon pepper

Other Ingredients:

2 pounds rack of lamb

3 lemons

¼ cup vinegar

1 cup BBQ sauce

Directions:

— Mix all spices together in a small bowl and then rub it over the meat.

— Then put the lamb on to baking dish and place inside the smoker to cook for 3 hours at 260°F.

— After 2 hours, open the smoker and take out the lamb.

— Mix lemon juice and BBQ sauce in a small bowl and pour over the lamb.

— Serve with this perfect BBQ glaze and enjoy.

— Enjoy!

Nutrition Facts per serving:

Calories 1256 and Daily Value*

Total Fat 71.6g 92%

Saturated Fat 35.6g 178%

Cholesterol 374mg 125%

Sodium 2753mg   120%

Total Carbohydrate 37.5g 14%

Dietary Fiber 2.6g   9%

Total Sugars 23.7g

Protein 107.7g

Calcium 117mg 9%

Iron 11mg 62%

Potassium 293mg 6%

Beef Jerky

Prep Time: 90 Minutes • Cooking Time: 4 Hour s • Servings: 4

Ingredients:

3 pounds thinly sliced beef

½ cup teriyaki sauce

2 cups brown sugar

2 tablespoons ginger paste

2 tablespoons onion powder

2 tablespoons lemon juice

Directions:

— First mix teriyaki sauce, brown sugar, ginger paste, and onion powder and lemon juice in a large bowl.

— Rub it over the beef.

— Let it stand for 1 hour in the fridge.

— Place apple wood chip into the smoker and let it preheat to 225 degrees F for 30 minutes.

— Now smoke the lamb by placing on the topmost rack of the smoker for 4 hours.

— Once done, serve.

Nutrition Facts per serving:

Calories 963 and Daily Value*

Total Fat 21.5g 28%

Saturated Fat 8.1g   41%

Cholesterol 304mg 101%

Sodium 1628mg 71%

Total Carbohydrate 81.6g 30%

Dietary Fiber 0.6g   2%
Total Sugars 76.9g
Protein 106.1g

Calcium 89mg 7%
Iron 66mg   364%
Potassium 1626mg 35%

Baby Back Ribs

Prep Time: 120 Minutes • Cooking Time: 90 Minutes • Servings: 3

Ingredients:

2 tablespoons salt

3 slabs baby back ribs

For The Sauce

3 cups tomato ketchup
¼ cup apple vinegar
3 tablespoons lemon juice

2 tablespoons garlic powder
½ tablespoon onion powder
2 tablespoons garlic pepper

Directions:

— Sprinkle 3 slabs of baby back ribs with the generous amount of salt.
— Combine all the sauce ingredients in a separate bowl and set aside for further use.
— Heat the electric smoker up to 260°F for 2 hours.
— Cover the meat with the glaze.
— Place it on a baking rack and smoker in the electric smoker for 90 minutes at 200 degrees F.
— Serve and enjoy by pouring the remaining sauce on top.

Nutrition Facts per serving:

Calories 596 and Daily Value*
Total Fat 34.2g 44%
Saturated Fat 12.1g 61%
Cholesterol 180mg 60%
Sodium 5953mg   259%
Total Carbohydrate 21.6g 8%

Dietary Fiber 0.6g   2%
Total Sugars 11.8g
Protein 53.1g
Calcium 10mg 1%
Iron 0mg 1%
Potassium 96mg   2%

Smoked Lamb Rib

Prep Time: 150 Minutes • Cooking Time: 3 Hours • Servings: 4

Ingredients:

2 pounds lamb rib chop

1 teaspoon black pepper

2 teaspoons BBQ Sauce

½ teaspoon salt

2 teaspoons apple vinegar

1 teaspoon thyme

2 teaspoons garlic powder

½ teaspoon onion powder

1 teaspoon ketchup

Directions:

— Combine all the listed ingredients in a bowl to make a glaze excluding meat. Pour the glaze on top of lamb rib and transfer it to the plastic zip lock bag. Place in freezer for 2 hours before start cooking.

— Afterward, put the lamb rib in a smoker and cook for 3 hours at 225 F.

— Brush the dripping on top and serve.

Nutrition Facts per serving:

Calories 394 and Daily Value*

Total Fat 20.1g 26%

Saturated Fat 7g 35%

Cholesterol 151mg 50%

Sodium 495mg 22%

Total Carbohydrate 3g 1%

Dietary Fiber 0.4g   1%

Total Sugars 1.4g

Protein 46.5g

Calcium 50mg 4%

Iron 4mg 23%

Potassium 37mg 1%

Beef Ribs

Prep Time: 30 Minutes • Cooking Time: 3 Hours • Servings: 2

Ingredients:

2 tablespoons brown sugar

2 tablespoons garlic, chopped

1 tablespoon paprika

2 tablespoons onion powder

2 pounds beef ribs

3 tablespoons lemon juice

Directions:

— Preheat smoker for 30 minutes at 200 degrees F.
— First mix first 4 ingredients together in a large bowl.
— Sprinkle the spice mixture over the pork ribs.
— Rub well for fine coating.
— Next, smoke it in an electric smoker for 3 hours at 250°F.
— After 2 hours, take out the ribs and pour lemon juice on top.
— Serve warm and enjoy.

Nutrition Facts per serving:

Calories 929 and Daily Value*
Total Fat 29g 37%
Saturated Fat 10.9g 55%
Cholesterol 405mg 135%
Sodium 312mg 14%
Total Carbohydrate 19.6g 7%

Dietary Fiber 2g 7%
Total Sugars 12.1g
Protein 139.5g
Calcium 61mg 5%
Iron 87mg 481%
Potassium 2047mg 44%

Steak with Butter

Prep Time: 90 Minutes • Cooking Time: 5 Hours 35 minutes • Servings: 4

Ingredients:

4 tablespoons salted butter
2 green onions, finely chopped.
½ tablespoon salt
1 tablespoon pepper
2 tablespoons parsley, fresh and
chopped
1 tablespoon smoked paprika, or to taste
2 tablespoons red wine vinegar
4 pounds steak

Directions:

— Place the butter in a bowl at room temperature until it softens.
— Now combine green onion, parsley, butter, salt, pepper, paprika and vinegar in a large bowl and mix. Add steaks and coat well.

— Cover this mixture into plastic wrap, then place it in the freezer until the butter hardens.
— Preheat the electric smoker to 225°f and add wood chips.
— Transfer the marinated steak into the aluminum foil tin and add to the smoker. Cook on high heat for 30 minutes.
— Turn the steak after every 5 minutes.
— Take out the meat from the smoker and cut it into the slices.
— Then again place the steaks into a smoker.
— Let it rest in the smoke for 5 more hours. Enjoy.

Nutrition Facts per serving:

Calories 1014 and Daily Value*
Total Fat 34.3g 44%
Saturated Fat 15.1g 76%
Cholesterol 439mg 146%
Sodium 1161mg   50%
Total Carbohydrate 1.9g   1%

Dietary Fiber 0.7g   3%
Total Sugars 0.2g
Protein 164.4g
Calcium 38mg 3%
Iron 16mg   88%
Potassium 1575mg 34%

Texas Brisket

Prep Time: 40 Minutes • Cooking Time: 90 Minutes • Servings: 1

Ingredients:

1 pound brisket
⅓ tablespoon salt
½ teaspoon black pepper
2 tablespoons lime juice

Directions:

— First mix salt, lime juice, and pepper in a small bowl.
— Pour it all over the brisket.
— Preheat smoker temperature to 225°F.

— Add the apple wood chips and wait until smoke started to build.
— Cook for about 90 minutes. Then serve.

Nutrition Facts per serving:

Calories 1266 and Daily Value*

Total Fat 100.4g 129%

Saturated Fat 40.2g201%

Cholesterol 361mg 120%

Sodium 2608mg 113%

Total Carbohydrate 7.4g 3%

Dietary Fiber 0.4g 1%

Total Sugars 1.5g

Protein 84.7g

Calcium 94mg 7%

Iron 7mg 41%

Potassium 102mg 2%

Smoked Leg of Lamb

Prep Time: 50 Minutes • Cooking Time: 90 Minutes • Servings: 1

Ingredients:

1 teaspoon coriander

½ teaspoon black pepper

1 teaspoon turmeric

2 teaspoons salt

½ teaspoon paprika

2 teaspoons vinegar

1 teaspoon onion powder

1 pound leg of lamb

Directions:

— Mix the coriander, black pepper, turmeric, salt, paprika, vinegar, and onion powder in a large bowl.
— Sprinkle the mixture all over the leg of lamb.
— Rub well for fine coating.
— Then put it in the smoker at 225°f for 90 minutes by adding apple wood chip for enhanced flavoring.
— After 3 hours, remove it from the electric smoker.
— Let stand at room temperature for 10 minutes.
— After 10 minutes cut it into small pieces.
— Enjoy!

Nutrition Facts per serving:

Calories 868 and Daily Value*

Total Fat 33.7g 43%

Saturated Fat 12g   60%

Cholesterol 408mg 136%

Sodium 4999mg   217%

Total Carbohydrate 4.7g   2%

Dietary Fiber 1.3g   5%

Total Sugars 1.1g

Protein 128.1g

Calcium 82mg 6%

Iron 12mg 68%

Potassium 1646mg 35%

Salted Brisket

Prep Time: 90 Minutes • Cooking Time: 3 Hours • Servings: 3

Ingredients:

2 teaspoons salt

1 teaspoon black pepper

1 teaspoon garlic paste

1 teaspoon ginger paste

½ teaspoon lemon juice

2 pinch five-spice powder

2 pounds of brisket

Directions:

— Cut the brisket into pieces.

— Mix all the remaining listed together in a bowl.

— Coat the brisket with the mixture. Put the brisket in the fridge for 1 hour.

— After 1 hour, transfer to the electric smoker and cook for 3 hours at 225 degrees F. Enjoy!

Nutrition Facts per serving:

Calories 835 and Daily Value*

Total Fat 67g 86%

Saturated Fat 26.8g 134%

Cholesterol 241mg 80%

Sodium 1738mg 76%

Total Carbohydrate 1.2g   0%

Dietary Fiber 0.3g   1%

Total Sugars 0.1g

Protein 56.4g

Calcium 60mg 5%

Iron 5mg 28%

Potassium 22mg

Maple Glazed Lamb

Prep Time: 7 Hours • Cooking Time: 3 and ½ Hours • Servings: 4

Ingredients:

2 pounds lamb

Brine Ingredients:

2 teaspoons salt

1 teaspoon vinegar

1 teaspoon garlic powder

1 teaspoon onion powder

4 cups water

Glaze Ingredients:

1 cup maple syrup

½ cup soy sauce

⅓ cup mustard

Salt and pepper, to taste

Directions:

— First, prepare the brine by mixing all the ingredients in a large pot.

— Cut the lamb into pieces. Submerge the lamb in brine mixture for 6 hours.

— Take out the lamb and pat dry. Let it dry at room temperature.

— Then put it in the smoker at 225°F for 3 hours.

— Meanwhile, mix all the glaze ingredients in a small mixing bowl.

— After 3 hours, drizzle maple glaze on top.

— Put the lamb again in a smoker at 175°F for half hour.

Nutrition Facts per serving:

Calories 711 and Daily Value*

Total Fat 20.6g 26%

Saturated Fat 6.2g 31%

Cholesterol 204mg 68%

Sodium 3148mg 137%

Total Carbohydrate 60.9g 22%

Dietary Fiber 2.3g 8%

Total Sugars 48.7g

Protein 69.2g

Calcium 168mg 13%

Iron 8mg 46%

Potassium 1097mg 23%

Spicy Baby Back Ribs

Prep Time: 30 Minutes • Cooking Time: 6 Hours • Servings: 6

Ingredients:

2 teaspoons salt

4 pounds slabs baby back ribs

1 teaspoon chili powder

1 teaspoon lemon pepper

½ teaspoon garlic pepper

1 teaspoon paprika

1 teaspoon black pepper

2 teaspoons lemon juice

2 teaspoons BBQ sauce

Directions:

— Cut the baby back ribs into pieces.

— Mix all the ingredients together in a bowl.

— Rub the mixture on the baby back ribs.

— Put the baby back ribs in the electric smoker at 225°F for 6 hours.

Nutrition Facts per serving:

Calories 1204 and Daily Value*

Total Fat 64.8g 83%

Saturated Fat 18.7g 94%

Cholesterol 271mg 90%

Sodium 3380mg   147%

Total Carbohydrate 65.3g 24%

Dietary Fiber 0.4g   1%

Total Sugars 64.6g

Protein 68.2g

Calcium 4mg 0%

Iron 0mg 1%

Potassium 27mg 1%

Mustard and Lime Flavored Brisket

Prep Time: 2 Hours • Cooking Time: 4 Hours 50 minutes • Servings: 3

Ingredients:

1 teaspoon paprika

1 teaspoon dried mustard

½ teaspoon thyme

2 teaspoons lime juice

1 teaspoon salt

3 pounds brisket

Directions:

— Mix paprika, dried mustard, thyme, lime juice, and salt together.
— Massage it all over the brisket for fine coating.
— Let it marinate in the refrigerator for 2 hours.
— Afterward, put the brisket in the electric smoker for cooking at 230°F for 4 hours 50 minutes. Serve and enjoy.

Nutrition Facts per serving:

Calories 1259 and Daily Value*
Total Fat 100.8g 129%
Saturated Fat 40.2g 201%
Cholesterol 361mg 120%
Sodium 1057mg   46%
Total Carbohydrate 3.4g   1%

Dietary Fiber 0.6g   2%
Total Sugars 0.6g
Protein 84.8g
Calcium 95mg 7%
Iron 8mg 43%
Potassium 59mg

Smoked Boneless Leg of Lamb

Prep Time: 70 Minutes • Cooking Time: 8 Hours • Servings: 8

Ingredients:

6 pounds legs of lamb, boneless
½ cup olive oil
4 teaspoons fresh rosemary, chopped

5 teaspoons fresh thyme, chopped
10 teaspoons BBQ sauce
1 teaspoon garlic powder

Directions:

— Rub ½ cup of olive oil on the leg of lamb.
— Mix chopped rosemary, garlic powder and fresh thyme in a bowl.
— Rub this mixture onto the leg of lamb.
— Put it in the refrigerator for 1 hour.
— After 1 hour, put the leg of lamb in the electric smoker at 225°F for 8 hours.
— After 2 hours, take out the lamb and drizzle BBQ sauce on top.
— Enjoy!

Nutrition Facts per serving:

Calories 1091 and Daily Value*

Total Fat 70.4g 90%

Saturated Fat 25.5g 128%

Cholesterol 288mg 96%

Sodium 667mg 29%

Total Carbohydrate 3.4g   1%

Dietary Fiber 0.6g   2%

Total Sugars 1.8g

Protein 246.9g

Calcium 61mg 5%

Iron 9mg 50%

Potassium 2976mg 63%

Jack Daniel's Meatloaf

Prep Time: 2 Hours 20 Minutes • Cooking Time: 6 Hours • Servings: 4

Ingredients:

4 pounds lamb meatloaf

Glaze Ingredients:

4 cloves garlic

2 teaspoons light soy sauce

2 tablespoons lemon juice

4 tablespoons brown sugar

½ tsp cayenne pepper

½ cup pineapple juice

½ cup water

½ cup teriyaki sauce

½ cup Jack Daniels Whiskey

1 tablespoon olive oil

Directions:

— Poke the lamb loaf with a fork.

— Combine all of the glaze ingredient in a bowl and brush it all over the meatloaf.

— Let it sit for few hours before cooking.

— Afterward, put the meatloaf in the electric smoker for 6 hours at 225°F.

— After every 30 minutes, baste the meat with the glaze.

— After 3 hours, take out the lamb and let it sit for 20 minutes at room temperature.

— Serve with the remaining glaze on top if desired.

Nutrition Facts per serving:

Calories 611 and Daily Value*

Total Fat 19.6g 25%

Saturated Fat 6.6g 33%

Cholesterol 100mg 33%

Sodium 2433mg 106%

Total Carbohydrate 58.3g 21%

Dietary Fiber 4.2g 15%

Total Sugars 18.1g

Protein 26.5g

Calcium 179mg 14%

Iron 4mg 22%

Potassium 84mg 2%

Beef Sirloin

Prep Time: 40 Minutes • Cooking Time: 4-5 Hours • Servings: 4

Ingredients:

4 pounds beef sirloin

Salt and black pepper, to taste

2 tablespoons vegetable oil

1 cup red wine

310 mL beef consommé

2 tablespoons butter

Directions:

— Sprinkle meat with salt, pepper, and rub vegetable oil on top.

— Afterward, put the meat in the electric smoker and cook for 4-5 hours at 220°F. Meanwhile, take a saucepan and add butter.

— Let it melt, and then pour in the red wine and let it cook until boil comes.

— Add the beef consommé.

— Once smooth and light, the sauce is ready. Turn off the heat.

— Take out the beef sirloin from the smoker and let it stand at room temperature for 20 minutes.

— Cut the meat and serve it by pouring sauce over the top.

Nutrition Facts per serving:

Calories 1032 and Daily Value*

Total Fat 40.9g 52%

Saturated Fat 15.7g 78%

Cholesterol 421mg 140%

Sodium 943mg 41%

Total Carbohydrate 3.1g 1%

Dietary Fiber 0g 0%

Total Sugars 1.5g

Protein 143.1g

Calcium 12mg 1%

Iron 86mg   475%

Potassium 1887mg 40%

Beef Prime Rib

Prep Time: 2 Hours • Cooking Time: 4 Hours 30 minutes • Servings: 4

Ingredients:

3 pounds beef prime rib, bone removed

2-3 tablespoons olive oil

½ tablespoon salt

½ tablespoon black pepper

1 teaspoon paprika

½ teaspoon cayenne pepper

½ teaspoon thyme

1 teaspoon onion powder

1 teaspoon rosemary

1 cup BBQ sauce

Directions:

— Combine the oil, salt, black pepper, paprika, cayenne pepper, thyme, onion powder, and rosemary in a bowl and mix well.

— Rub it gently over prime rib. Let it sit for a few hours.

— Meanwhile, preheat the smoker to 200 degrees F for 2 hours.

— Then, smoke the meat inside the smoker for 4 hours and a half hour.

— Afterward, serve it with the BBQ sauce.

Nutrition Facts per serving:

Calories 1560 and Daily Value*

Total Fat 126.9g 163%

Saturated Fat 50.4g 252%

Cholesterol 286mg 95%

Sodium 1794mg   78%

Total Carbohydrate 24.4g 9%

Dietary Fiber 1.1g   4%

Total Sugars 16.6g

Protein 75.6g

Calcium 66mg 5%

Iron 7mg 41%

Potassium 1266mg 27%

Smoked T-bone steak

Prep Time: 90 Minutes • Cooking Time: 4 Hours • Servings: 4

Ingredients:

4(16 ounces) t-bone steaks
1 cup prime rib rub mixture
1 cup mozzarella cheese

Directions:

— Rub the meat with prime rib rub and wrap into plastic wrap.
— Then put in a fridge for 1 hour.
— Preheat the smoker to 225°F for 30 minutes, by adding apple wood chips.
— Transfer the steaks to the larger baking rack, and place it inside the smoker for cooking.
— Next, insert the probe thermometer inside the meat for heat measurements.
— Cook the steaks until internal temperature reaches 200°degrees F.
— Top with mozzarella cheese.

Nutrition Facts per serving:

Calories 921 and Daily Value*
Total Fat 41.9g 54%
Saturated Fat 15.9g 80%
Cholesterol 244mg 81%
Sodium 503mg 22%
Total Carbohydrate 0.9g 0%
Dietary Fiber 0g 0%
Total Sugars 0g
Protein 126.1g
Calcium 23mg 2%
Iron 17mg   92%
Potassium 1483mg 32%

Delicious Rib-Eye Steak

Prep Time: 2 Hours • Cooking Time: 4 Hours • Servings: 4

Ingredients:

4 rib-eye steak, 2-inches thick

2 cups sharp cheddar cheese, grated

Spice Ingredients:

1 teaspoon black pepper

3 tablespoons chipotle powder

½ tablespoon paprika

½ cup olive oil

Directions:

— Combine the entire spice ingredient in a bowl and rub it all over the meat.
— Let it sit for few hours before cooking. Afterward, put the steaks in the electric smoker for 4 hours at 225°F. After 4 hours take out the lamb and sprinkle cheese on top. Let the cheese get melted, and then serve.

Nutrition Facts per serving:

Calories 1623 and Daily Value*

Total Fat 136.4g 175%

Saturated Fat 51.7g 258%

Cholesterol 421mg 140%

Sodium 1006mg 44%

Total Carbohydrate 3.8g 1%

Dietary Fiber 0.5g   2%

Total Sugars 1.9g

Protein 22.3g

Calcium 411mg 32%

Iron 8mg 44%

Potassium 82mg 2%

Garlic Mustard Smoked Beef Tenderloin

Prep Time: 5 Hour • Cooking Time: 3 Hours 30 Minutes • Servings: 3

Ingredients:

3 pounds beef tenderloin
2 sticks or cubes of butter

Ingredients for Rub:

2 tablespoons black peppercorns

2 tablespoons white peppercorns

1 tablespoon sea salt

Ingredients for the Baste:

10 cloves fresh garlic, minced

⅓ cup parsley, chopped

½ cup rosemary, chopped

2 teaspoons English mustard

2 teaspoons honey

2 tablespoons of olive oil

6 ounces of Armagnac or brandy

Directions:

— Combine all the basting Ingredients in a large pot and submerge the beef in it for 4 hours.

— Afterward, take out the tenderloin from the basting mixture and let it sit at room temperature.

— Mix the entire rub ingredient in a small bowl and rub it gently all over the beef tenderloin for fine coating.

— Smoke on top most racks for half hour at 225 degrees F by adding apple wood chips.

— Afterward, transfer it to the plate and rub 2 sticks of butter.

— Seal it with aluminum foil and cook for 3 hours at 225°F.

— Remove from smoker and immediately serve.

— Enjoy.

Nutrition Facts per serving:

Calories 1692 and Daily Value*

Total Fat 113.6g 146%

Saturated Fat 56.6g 283%

Cholesterol 579mg 193%

Sodium 2586mg   112%

Total Carbohydrate 16.6g 6%

Dietary Fiber 5.7g   20%

Total Sugars 4.1g

Protein 133.8g

Calcium 260mg   20%

Iron 14mg   75%

Potassium 1862mg 40%

Made in the USA
San Bernardino, CA
28 June 2018